QUESTIONS & ANSWERS:
CRIMINAL PROCEDURE —
PROSECUTION AND ADJUDICATION

QUESTIONS & ANSWERS:
CRIMINAL PROCEDURE —
PROSECUTION AND ADJUDICATION

Multiple Choice and Short Answer
Questions and Answers

Third Edition

NEIL P. COHEN
Retired Distinguished Service Professor of Law and W.P. Toms Professor of Law
The University of Tennessee College of Law

MICHAEL J. BENZA
Senior Instructor of Law
Case Western Reserve University School of Law

WAYNE A. LOGAN
Gary & Sallyn Pajcic Professor of Law
Florida State University College of Law

CAROLINA ACADEMIC PRESS
Durham, North Carolina

ISBN: 978-1-6328-4954-0

Carolina Academic Press, LLC
700 Kent Street
Durham, NC 27701
Telephone (919) 489-7486
Fax (919) 493-5668
www.caplaw.com

Printed in the United States of America

ABOUT THE AUTHORS

Neil P. Cohen is a Retired Distinguished Service Professor of Law and W.P. Toms Professor of Law at the University of Tennessee College of Law. He taught evidence, criminal law, and criminal procedure. Professor Cohen is the author or editor of 13 books published in over 30 editions, and numerous law review articles. These publications include treatises on evidence and criminal law and casebooks on criminal law and criminal procedure. He has also participated in drafting state rules of criminal law, criminal procedure, and evidence. His practice experience includes both criminal defense and prosecution. Professor Cohen has received many awards for teaching, scholarship, and public service. His memberships include the American Law Institute.

Michael J. Benza received his Bachelor of Arts (1986) and law degree (1992) from Case Western Reserve University. He also received a Master of Arts degree in Clinical Psychology (1988) from Pepperdine University. He was the 1992 Biskind Fellow from CWRU School of Law and spent a year working for the Legal Resources Centre, a civil and human rights law firm in South Africa. Upon returning to the States, he spent four years in the Capital Defense Unit at the Office of the Ohio Public Defender. He was assistant counsel at the Cleveland Bar Association working with the Certified Grievance Committee as well as other committees. Professor Benza teaches Criminal Law, Criminal Procedure I and II, Death Penalty Issues, the Death Penalty Lab, Federal Prisoner Rights, International Perspectives on the Death Penalty, as well as coaching the International Criminal Court moot court team and he previously coached the Mock Trial team. The Student Bar Association selected Professor Benza as the Professor of the Year in 2007, 2008, 2009, 2010, 2011, 2013, and 2014. In 2009, Professor Benza was elected as an alumni member to the Society of Benchers. Professor Benza continues to represent death row inmates in state courts and federal *habeas* proceedings. He has litigated capital cases in state trial courts, state appellate and post-conviction courts, and federal courts including arguing *Smith v. Spisak*, 558 U.S. 139 (2010), before the Supreme Court of the United States.

Wayne A. Logan, Gary & Salllyn Pajcic Professor at the Florida State University College of Law, teaches and writes in the areas of Criminal Law, Criminal Procedure, and Sentencing. He is the recipient of a university-wide teaching award and is the author of several dozen law review articles, with work appearing in such publications as the *Georgetown Law Journal, Michigan Law Review*, the *Pennsylvania Law Review*, and the *Vanderbilt Law Review*. His most recent book, *Knowledge as Power: Criminal Registration and Community Notification Laws in America* (Stanford University Press, 2009), was cited by the U.S. Supreme Court in *United States v. Kebodeaux* (2013). Professor Logan is an elected member of the American Law Institute and a past chair of the Criminal Justice Section of the Association of American Law Schools.

PREFACE

This book will assist your learning and exam preparation for the criminal procedure prosecution-adjudication course and for the bar exam. The subject matter of the book extends to all major subjects covered in this course. The book contains both multiple choice questions and answers, and short essay questions and answers.

As the following Table of Contents reflects, the book covers discretion to prosecute, bail, complaint, initial appearance, preliminary hearing, grand jury, indictments and informations, plea bargaining, joinder and severance, motion practice, discovery, time limitations, jurisdiction and venue, the jury trial, double jeopardy, sentencing (including death penalty), and post-conviction remedies.

We suggest that you answer the question before consulting our answer. This approach will aid your learning by alerting you to areas in which you need to improve your understanding.

The "short essays" in this book are likely longer than you will find in other volumes in this series. The reason is that the type of question that will best prepare you for an exam is rarely susceptible to a one-paragraph answer.

We have tried to balance brevity with the need to provide realistic, useful questions. Our practice has been to err on the side of usefulness, resulting in some longer discussions. While the answers to our short essay questions vary in length, none is more than three paragraphs. And, unless otherwise indicated, the question can at times be answered in one paragraph (perhaps as long as 12 sentences). But do not fret if your answer comes in slightly longer or shorter than our answer. As long as the substance is adequate, your answer is just fine. If your answer is longer, you may want to consider whether you could have given a shorter response. On some law school exams, where time is limited, brevity may be a valuable asset.

March 2016

Professor Neil Philip Cohen
San Rafael, California

Professor Michael Benza
Case Western Reserve University
School of Law

Professor Wayne A. Logan
Florida State University
College of Law

TABLE OF CONTENTS

TABLE OF CONTENTS

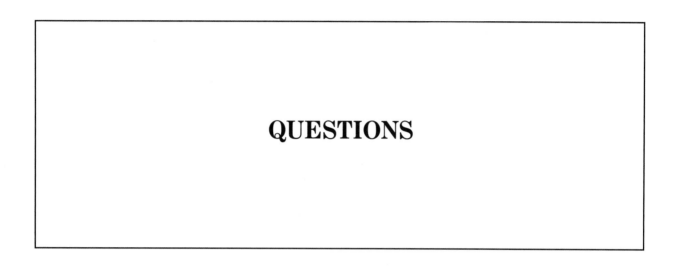

QUESTIONS

A defendant is prosecuted in federal court for several felonies involving kidnapping.

1.   If all significant federal procedures are followed in the case, which of the following would occur THIRD chronologically?

    (A) initial appearance.

    (B) arrest.

    (C) grand jury.

    (D) preliminary examination (also known as a preliminary hearing).

The Governor's niece, Stephanie Neece, a student at the local college, got drunk at a fraternity party and drove in her new Porsche to a friend's house to continue partying. On the way, Neece's car collided with that of Takisha Curry, killing Curry and her one-year-old baby sleeping in the back seat.

The local prosecutor investigated the case and charged Neece only with drunk driving. Curry's family is furious, wanting Neece to be charged with two counts of reckless homicide. The prosecutor explained the decision: "I have known Steph for many years and she is a good kid. She feels bad about the accident and has apologized to the Curry family. No need to ruin Stephanie's life over one stupid mistake."

Curry's family has consulted you about filing suit against the prosecutor to force her to file reckless homicide charges against Neece.

2. If a suit were filed, the judge would likely:

   (A) issue the injunction compelling the district attorney to prosecute Neece.

   (B) empanel a grand jury and order the case presented to them.

   (C) appoint a special prosecutor.

   (D) dismiss the action.

3. In which of the following scenarios are Federal Rule of Criminal Procedure 3 and 4.1's requirements (as amended by case law) for a valid complaint NOT violated?

(A) FBI agent Chu submitted a sworn, signed statement that "Defendant Amy Bierman committed an act of terrorism against the United States" and a federal magistrate judge signed the complaint, but no one else signed it.

(B) FBI agent LeBaron appeared before a magistrate judge in a major narcotics case. She told the magistrate the essential facts of the case, and the magistrate suggested how to word the charged offense. The FBI agent wrote the statement containing the essential facts of the charge as suggested by the magistrate but did not sign it, and hurried back to the U.S. Attorney's Office, where the supervising Assistant U.S. Attorney signed a separate document stating simply, "I have read Agent LeBaron's statement and approve it." The magistrate judge signed the complaint.

(C) FBI agent O'Sullivan submitted a written, sworn statement to a magistrate judge containing the essential facts and the charged offenses, using language that substantially mirrored the words in the federal criminal law allegedly violated. The magistrate judge cornered an Assistant U.S. Attorney, who happened to be in the federal courtroom, and who read and signed the statement.

(D) FBI agent Cook submitted a written statement to a *state* judge because all the federal magistrate judges were at a conference for federal judicial personnel. The written statement contained the essential facts and the charged offenses. Since no U.S. Attorney was available, a secretary in the U.S. Attorney's office signed the name of the United States Attorney for the District. The state judge signed the complaint.

You are a federal agent who just arrested Sophie, a U.S. Postal Service mail carrier, for theft of mail from letters addressed to people on her mail route. The arrest occurred at 3:30 p.m. on August 3rd in the area covered by the United States District Court for the Eastern District of State A. You know that Sophie is entitled to an initial appearance under Federal Rule of Criminal Procedure 5.

4. Assume that the arrest was made on the basis of a valid arrest warrant issued the day before the arrest and based on a complaint filed by a federal undercover drug agent who had followed Sophie on her route for several days and observed her take checks from envelopes and then discard the envelopes, some of which were retrieved by agents. Under Rule 5, where and when should you take Sophie before a magistrate?

ANSWER:

5. Same facts as above except the crime occurred in the area covered by the Eastern District of State A, but the arrest was 10 miles away in the Western District of State A. Where must the initial appearance be held?

ANSWER:

6. Changing the facts, how would the procedural requirements be affected if the arrest were made without a warrant?

ANSWER:

7. At a federal initial appearance in a felony case, under Rule 5(d) the court must inform the defendant of which of the following?

(A) the complaint and any affidavit.

(B) the circumstances, if any, for obtaining pretrial release.

(C) the defendant's right to remain silent.

(D) all of above.

8. The United States Constitution deals with the concept of bail in the Eighth Amendment. What practice is barred by this provision?

    (A) excessive bail.

    (B) denial of bail.

    (C) setting money bail on indigent defendants.

    (D) allowing professional bail bonding companies to use excessive force to detain bail jumpers.

Marvin, an accountant, was arrested for embezzlement. He was taken before Judge Mai Fong who set a $5,000 bond but was willing to consider other options. As an accountant, Marvin wants to know how much each option would cost him out of pocket if he attends all hearings in the case.

9. Which of the following release options would cost him the MOST money in the long run?

    (A) cash bond.

    (B) surety bond using a bail bonding company.

    (C) property bond.

    (D) unsecured bond.

10. Wylie is arrested for shoplifting from a local discount store and taken to jail. This jail uses a bail/bond schedule in some release decisions, including shoplifting. What is a bail or bond schedule and what are its advantages and disadvantages?

ANSWER:

11. The 1984 Federal Bail Reform Act directs the judge assessing release options to consider which of the following factors?

    (A) safety of the community.

    (B) safety of any person other than the accused.

    (C) appearance for trial.

(D) all of above.

Monique is arrested for the felony of illegally purchasing and using federal food stamps. This is her first arrest. She is taken before a federal magistrate judge to arrange for her release pending trial.

12. According to the Bail Reform Act, the option most preferred for Monique is:

(A) release on the condition that she make immediate restitution.

(B) release on personal recognizance or unsecured appearance bond.

(C) release on secured bond.

(D) temporary detention until the parties work out arrangements guaranteeing appearance at all hearings.

In assessing whether a person charged with a federal crime poses a serious risk of injuring a witness, requiring continued detention because no condition will reasonably assure the safety of the witness, the Bail Reform Act of 1984 establishes a standard of proof the judge must use in this decision.

13. What is the standard of proof for this determination?

(A) probable cause.

(B) preponderance of the evidence.

(C) clear and convincing evidence.

(D) beyond a reasonable doubt.

You are a federal appellate judge presiding in the appeal of a case involving Carlos Fuentes who is in jail awaiting trial for holding hostages in a federal building at gunpoint. Fuentes was a former police lieutenant who allegedly took the hostages to make the point that his law enforcement colleagues had framed him for embezzling from the police department and killing an undercover police investigator. Fuentes had threatened to "get even with those lying suckers."

At a detention hearing, defense counsel argued that Fuentes should be released until the trial because he has long-term community ties, a steady job, and no criminal record. The federal magistrate judge rejected these arguments and ordered Fuentes to remain in jail until the trial in three months. In giving her judgment, the magistrate judge said, "I believe your client will appear for trial but he is a threat to the safety of the community because this fallen angel seemed pretty comfortable pointing a gun at these civil servants and making serious threats to good people," pointing to several individuals sitting in the courtroom.

Defense counsel has appealed this decision, based on a prediction of future criminality, arguing its constitutionally infirm because the only reason a person should be detained is a reasonable likelihood that he or she will not appear for trial. Otherwise, the presumption of innocence is meaningless.

14. How will you rule on the appeal?

ANSWER:

Your client just was convicted of two serious drug counts and sentenced to 10 years in federal prison. You think the trial judge committed reversible error in admitting records obtained in an unconstitutional search. You have appealed the conviction but know that the process will be lengthy. You want your client released on bail pending resolution of the appeal if at all possible.

15. Which of the following is the correct standard for release pending appeal under the 1984 Bail Reform Act?

    (A) Release pending appeal is not authorized because of the high likelihood of escape.

    (B) The convicted person must be detained unless defense counsel can show beyond a reasonable doubt that the person will appear at all future proceedings and is not a threat to the safety of another person or the community.

    (C) The appeal must raise a substantial question of law or fact likely to result in a reversal or an order for a new trial.

    (D) The trial court must set a bail amount, though it can be quite high, because of the Eighth Amendment's bail guarantee.

16. The 1984 Bail Reform Act authorizes the detention of a material witness to ensure the witness will testify. When would this detention NOT be authorized?

    (A) when the witness's testimony could be adequately secured by a deposition.

    (B) when the witness promises, under oath, to appear at the trial.

    (C) when counsel for the witness certifies under oath that the witness will appear at the trial.

    (D) when the witness is actually served with a subpoena requiring presence at the trial, under penalty of a contempt citation for failing to appear.

You have just been appointed to a state bar committee charged with making recommendations to improve criminal procedure. Your subcommittee is dealing with the preliminary hearing covered by Rule 5.1 of the Federal Rules of Criminal Procedure and applicable in your jurisdiction. You have been doing a lot of reading about the preliminary hearing.

17. Under Rule 5.1, when is a preliminary hearing REQUIRED in a felony case?

(A) after a defendant is indicted for a felony.

(B) after a prosecutor files an information charging a felony.

(C) for any felony or misdemeanor if incarceration is possible.

(D) for any felony unless the defendant has waived the hearing or there has been an indictment.

18. Under Rule 5.1, when is a preliminary hearing NOT required?

(A) when the prosecution waives the hearing.

(B) when an indictment is issued for the crime.

(C) when the defendant asks for a jury trial.

(D) when defense counsel abuses the hearing and tries to use it for discovery.

19. Which of the following is NOT TRUE about the federal preliminary hearing?

(A) it is an adversary proceeding in which a prosecutor and criminal defense lawyer will likely participate.

(B) the accused may testify.

(C) the decision is made by a jury of 12.

(D) the accused may cross-examine prosecution witnesses.

You have studied Rule 5.1 of the Federal Rules of Criminal Procedure in preparation for your upcoming subcommittee meeting.

20. Which one of the following provisions is actually in Rule 5.1?

(A) evidence obtained in violation of the Constitution may be admissible.

(B)   the prosecution cannot admit hearsay information in violation of Federal Rules of Evidence, which apply in full measure in preliminary hearings.

(C)   if the preliminary hearing judge finds no probable cause that the defendant committed the charged offense, the judge should nevertheless order the accused to remain in custody until the grand jury hears the case because the defendant may abscond before the grand jury can act.

(D)   the judge can hold the preliminary examination 30 days after the defendant's initial appearance regardless of whether the defendant is in custody.

You are a judge in a jurisdiction that has criminal procedure rules identical to the Federal Rules of Criminal Procedure. You just conducted a preliminary hearing in a hotly contested case involving a fight in a bar. There were witnesses for both sides on the issue whether the defendant struck the victim in self-defense. The case is difficult because all the witnesses seemed to be credible.

21.   Which of the following would be the most accurate statement of the law of preliminary hearings?

(A)   the standard of proof is probable cause that a crime was committed and that the accused committed that crime.

(B)   the standard of proof is guilt beyond a reasonable doubt.

(C)   the fact that all the witnesses were credible means that the defense did not prove that the defendant was innocent.

(D)   the prosecution must use its best available witnesses rather than choosing not to in order to prevent the defense from discovering what their testimony will be at trial.

In an insider trading case, federal government agents intercepted and recorded cell phone conversations, but in violation of Supreme Court decisions under the Fourth Amendment, did not get a search warrant to do so. Moreover, some of the conversations involved multiple hearsay statements not admissible under the evidence rules. The prosecution wants to know whether these recorded conversations may be used at the preliminary hearing later in the week.

22.   Assess the admissibility of the cell phone conversations in the federal preliminary hearing.

ANSWER:

You are a district attorney given a case involving an assault in a domestic violence assault. The victim — wife first complained to the police that her husband, Samuel Pierson, had beaten her, then she changed her mind and asked that the case be dropped. She asked again that the case be dropped when she testified before the grand jury, which declined to indict. Since the victim did not want to prosecute and the grand jury refused to indict, you decided to abandon the case.

The local newspaper has now published a series of articles on domestic violence and is urging that all domestic violence perpetrators be prosecuted "to the full extent of the law." The paper cites studies showing that jurisdictions that have "mandatory prosecution" rules have lower incidents of domestic violence. You have now changed your mind and think you should prosecute such cases even when the victim does not want to do so.

You have identified four options with regard to proceeding in the above case:

   I. Resubmit the matter to a different grand jury.

  II. Do nothing. The grand jury decision acts as an acquittal and further prosecution is barred by the Double Jeopardy Clause.

III. Ask Mr. Pierson's lawyer for permission to proceed by information.

IV. Ask the same grand jury to reconsider.

  23. In a typical non-federal jurisdiction with no statutes or rule on point, which of the following statements accurately reflects your choices among the above options?

      (A) I only.

      (B) II only.

      (C) I and III only.

      (D) I, III, and IV only.

On Sunday at midnight, the transit workers began to strike, effectively halting all public transportation in the city. A grand jury has been hearing cases for several months and is nearing the end of its docket. While some grand jurors are unable to get to the federal court one morning because of the strike, many were able to walk or get a ride to the courthouse and wanted to continue working on their caseload by hearing witnesses and resolving cases.

  24. Under Rule 6 of the Federal Rules of Criminal Procedure, what is the minimum number of grand jurors who must vote to indict in order to return a valid federal indictment?

      (A) 24.

      (B) 12.

(C) 9.

(D) 16.

The supply room in a federal court is preparing to order one new notepad for each of the grand jurors in one jury room.

25. How many notepads must be ordered if each federal grand juror is given one notepad and if the maximum number of grand jurors appears on the day the pads are distributed?

(A) 12.

(B) 23.

(C) 24.

(D) 40.

A defense attorney received a copy of an indictment charging her client with wire fraud. She later learned that when a witness named Henrico Hernandez testified before the grand jury, he did so with a Spanish interpreter because he did not speak any English. The defense attorney also learned that the Assistant United States Attorney and a court reporter were present while Hernandez was testifying. Knowing that grand jury proceedings are secret, the defense attorney wants to challenge the indictment because of the presence of these three people when Hernandez testified.

26. What is the likely result of the challenge?

ANSWER:

27. In federal court, which of the following DOES NOT remove the defendant's right to a preliminary hearing under Rule 5.1?

(A) the defendant is indicted by a grand jury.

(B) the defendant is charged with a misdemeanor and agrees to trial before a magistrate judge.

(C) the defendant requests jury trial.

(D) the government files a valid information for a felony.

28. Which of the following groups of people are NOT subject to a general obligation of secrecy about grand jury proceedings?

(A) grand jury witnesses.

(B) grand jurors.

(C) grand jury interpreters.

    (D) grand jury court reporters.

29. Who among the following individuals is NOT specifically authorized to discover information about which witnesses testified in a specific grand jury proceeding?

    (A) an attorney for the government for use in the performance of her job.

    (B) an investigator assisting a government attorney in the performance of her job.

    (C) state government officials who are assisting a federal attorney in investigating violation of federal law.

    (D) the person indicted in that proceeding.

30. Which of the following is NOT TRUE about a federal grand jury?

    (A) the grand jury may consider evidence barred by the Federal Rules of Evidence.

    (B) the grand jury may issue an indictment that is sealed by the magistrate judge until the accused is arrested.

    (C) the witness's testimony is not recorded by a court reporter or device in order to preserve grand jury secrecy.

    (D) the grand jury's voting and deliberations are not recorded by a court reporter or device in order to preserve grand jury secrecy.

31. A Bill of Particulars is:

   (A) an itemized statement of amounts owed for professional legal services.

   (B) a request by the government for more details about the defendant's likely defenses so the government can be fully prepared for trial.

   (C) a request by defense counsel for additional information about the crimes alleged in an indictment.

   (D) an order by the judge for information about the likely evidence to be used by each side and is designed to assist the court in predicting how long the trial will take.

32. Which of the following is CORRECT about a Bill of Particulars under Federal Rule 7(f)?

   (A) The court may require defense counsel to file a Bill of Particulars within 14 days after arraignment or at a later date.

   (B) Once any party files a Bill of Particulars, it may not be amended because doing so would be unfair to the other party.

   (C) A Bill of Particulars amends an indictment so that even a faulty indictment would become valid.

   (D) The court may, but is not required to, order the government to file a Bill of Particulars.

You are the attorney for a former Wall Street investment banker who has been indicted for committing securities fraud "in connection with seven transactions" he handled while employed at a bank. Your client informs you that over the course of the 25 years he worked at the bank, he was involved in thousands of transactions and the indictment does not indicate what seven transactions are allegedly fraudulent.

33. Why might it be helpful for defense counsel to request a Bill of Particulars?

ANSWER:

You are a prosecutor in a jurisdiction that has criminal procedure rules similar to those in federal courts. You want to use the most efficient procedures possible. Recently, there has been a large number of misdemeanor cases as local law enforcement personnel have cracked down on gambling and prostitution. Which of the following procedures would be adequate to permit a trial for the misdemeanors:

34. You may proceed with the misdemeanor trials by:

     (A) information.

     (B) indictment.

     (C) complaint.

     (D) all of above.

35. Which of the following is NOT required for a valid federal indictment?

     (A) that it be in writing.

     (B) that it cite the statute allegedly violated.

     (C) that it be signed by the defense attorney.

     (D) that it be signed by an attorney for the government.

You represent a man charged with rape. He has told you an incredible story how the alleged victim actually seduced him and the sex was consensual. You are skeptical to say the least. However, your investigator located the victim's diary, which completely corroborated your client's version of the incident. You take the diary to the district attorney and ask that it be given to the grand jury considering the rape charges. The prosecutor refuses to do so, telling you, "Use it at trial if you think it is so important." The grand jury indicts your client for rape.

36. You want to challenge the indictment because of the prosecutor's actions in depriving the grand jury of very relevant and available defense evidence. Assess the likely result based on the Federal Rules of Criminal Procedure.

ANSWER:

You work for a subcommittee of the United States House of Representatives and are exploring ways to streamline federal criminal procedure so that victims do not have to wait as long to obtain justice. One possible measure is to reduce the cases where an indictment is necessary because your research has found that the use of indictments may delay a case for 4–6 months.

37. Under current federal criminal procedure, which of the following crimes does NOT have to be initiated by an indictment?

     (A) a crime punishable by life imprisonment.

     (B) a crime punishable by two years in prison but the defendant is convicted and sentenced to two years of probation and never actually goes to prison.

     (C) a crime punishable by a maximum of 12 months imprisonment.

(D)   a crime that is a felony.

You represent a mob-connected defendant charged in state court with extortion, a serious felony. The prosecution has used several undercover agents in the investigation and does not want their identities known. There have been several instances recently when confidential information presented to the grand jury was somehow leaked to the press. To maximize the likelihood that secrecy could be maintained, the state prosecutor decided to proceed by information rather than indictment. State law gives the prosecutor the option of using either an indictment or an information for non-capital felonies.

38.   You want to challenge the constitutionality of the state's use of an information rather than an indictment for a serious felony. You know federal procedure would require an indictment in this situation. Assess your chances of successfully challenging this practice by state authorities.

ANSWER:

39. Which of the following is ordinarily NOT required for a valid pretrial motion under Rule 47 of the Federal Rules of Criminal Procedure, assuming the judge has not authorized a departure from the requirements of this rule?

    (A) that it be in writing if made before a trial or hearing.

    (B) that it state the grounds on which it is based.

    (C) that it be supported by an affidavit.

    (D) that it be served on all parties.

You represent a mob boss accused of many violent crimes as well as a number of conspiracies. You expect the federal trial to last for months and to involve as many as a hundred motions. The judge handling the case is known to require adherence to all rules of procedure. You do not want to file untimely motions because this judge has dismissed some simply because of a tardy submission.

40. Which of the following motions does NOT have to be raised before trial under Rule 12?

    (A) Motion to admit certain evidence.

    (B) Motion to Suppress Evidence.

    (C) Motion to Sever Charges.

    (D) Motion to Dismiss Indictment for Improper Selection of Grand Jurors.

You receive the following memo from the judge who just hired you as her law clerk:

> To: New Law Clerk
>
> From: Federal District Judge Neophyte
>
> Re: Motions in Criminal Cases
>
> Dear New Law Clerk,
>
> Since I was appointed to the bench last month, I've been reading over the Federal Rules of Criminal Procedure but am a bit perplexed. I've never handled a criminal case before in my law practice and I couldn't find any rule that concerns specific types of motions that are filed in criminal cases. Please prepare a short list for me of the general types of routine motions I can expect in criminal cases. I know your response will have to be quite general.

41. How do you respond to the Judge's memo?

ANSWER:

You are a federal prosecutor scheduled to begin a complex and lengthy criminal antitrust case in exactly a month. Today is Friday and you have a motion hearing on Monday to resolve all outstanding motions. Late that Friday afternoon, a runner from defense counsel's law office appears at your office and serves you with a Motion to Suppress Defendant's Confession. You were quite surprised since defense counsel had not hinted that the confession would be challenged and you can think of no reason why it should be excluded, but it will take a lot of research to gather case support for your position. The confession is extremely important to your case.

Since all outstanding motions are to be heard on Monday, you think it likely that this one will be as well. You know that the judge does not like continuances and is already unhappy about the time this matter has taken so far and will be consumed in the coming months.

42. What are your options for submitting a timely reply to the defense motion?

ANSWER:

You represent a client accused of rape that allegedly occurred when he slipped a drug in the drink of a woman he met at a bar, then took her to his car and sexually assaulted her. Your client told you the woman asked for the drug and took it voluntarily, then suggested they go to his car where they had consensual sexual relations. Your investigator discovered that your client had two previous complaints for giving women drugged drinks without their knowledge and then having sexual relations with them while they were impaired by the drug. He served a three-year sentence for one of these charges.

43. What would be the best way to increase the likelihood that those details about the previous incidents stay out of the upcoming rape trial?

(A) at trial, make a timely and specific objection any time you believe a witness or prosecutor is about to broach the subject.

(B) at trial, avoid asking questions that would trigger consideration of evidence about the previous incidents.

(C) file a motion in limine to bar any reference to the previous incidents.

(D) nothing because your client's acts are admissible because they are so similar to the one at issue.

Mary Lawford was convicted of tax evasion in federal court. In a written pretrial motion, her defense lawyer asked the prosecutor to provide the defense with an F.B.I. report concerning an investigation of a third person. Defense counsel thinks perhaps the third person was actually responsible for the tax crime. The prosecutor never responded to the motion and it was not discussed in a hearing or ruled on by the magistrate judge. You are handling the appeal and have raised the government's failure to turn over the F.B.I. report about the third person's possible involvement in the crime.

44. How will the appellate court likely treat this motion?

(A) arguments raised by the motion are probably waived because no disposition was ever reached at the trial court level.

(B) because the F.B.I. reports were not introduced at trial, failure to consider the motion is harmless error.

(C) the cause should be remanded to the trial court for a hearing on the motion and any effect it might have on the trial outcome.

(D) the appellate court should consider the motion on the merits and attempt to determine if the non-disclosed report would have had any real bearing on the outcome of the trial.

You are head prosecutor in a jurisdiction following the Federal Rules of Criminal Procedure. Your office rules mandate that a written response be filed for each defense motion. However, recently your small office (only seven lawyers) has been swamped with motions filed in three significant pending cases and your lawyers simply do not have time to prepare written responses to each and handle their other cases as well. You are quite sure, however, that two of the three cases will never go to trial since ongoing plea discussions suggest there will be guilty pleas (and therefore no trial) for both.

You were discussing this problem with a prosecutor from another jurisdiction who said that her office usually does not file written responses to motions, but rather simply mounts arguments against them at the motion hearing. Written responses are filed only when absolutely necessary. You are considering advocating that your office adopt a similar procedure of filing written responses only when really necessary. If you do stop filing written responses to motions, what do you think the local judges will do since they carefully adhere to all criminal procedure rules?

45. Using the Federal Rules of Criminal Procedure (and not any local rules), the court should:

(A) grant all the defense motions as the prosecutor waived any objection for failure to file a timely written response.

(B) scold the prosecutor but grant a one-week continuance and demand that written responses to the motions be filed forthwith.

(C) consider the motions on their merits but refuse to allow the prosecutor to offer any objection or rebuttal on the record.

(D) consider the motions on the merits after hearing any arguments from the prosecutor.

You are a criminal defense lawyer representing a politician charged with using campaign contributions for personal expenses in violation of federal election law. Your defense is that the money was for legitimate consulting fees. Trial is going extremely well. Your witnesses are quite credible and the government's proof was weak to begin with and the key government witness essentially testified in a way very helpful to your client. You think a Motion for a Judgment of Acquittal would have a good chance of being granted.

46. What is the timing for filing this particular motion and when must the federal judge rule on it, under the Federal Rules of Criminal Procedure?

ANSWER:

47. Same facts as above. Assume the trial judge grants the Motion for a Judgment of Acquittal after the jury reached a verdict of guilty. Which of the following is TRUE?

    (A) because the case was resolved by the jury's guilty verdict, an appellate court may not reverse the trial court's decision because of the Double Jeopardy Clause.

    (B) the trial judge should decide whether a conditional Motion for New Trial should be granted if the appellate court reverses the decision to grant the Motion for a Judgment of Acquittal.

    (C) if the trial court grants a conditional Motion for New Trial, hinging on the appellate court's reversal of the trial court's decision on the Motion for Judgment of Acquittal, the case is not considered to be final since appellate reversal is possible.

    (D) the case is not appealable by the government since the court's granting of the Motion for Judgment of Acquittal ends the case pursuant to the Double Jeopardy Clause.

Your client, Benjamin Farlow, was just convicted of killing Laurie Villow and sentenced to life imprisonment. The killer bludgeoned Villow to death with a tire iron that was recovered from the crime scene. The tire iron contained no helpful DNA or other evidence. The jury disbelieved your client's alibi witness, his mother who testified that he was at her house watching television the entire evening that the crime occurred.

This week you read about a brand new DNA test that could assess the DNA from sweat left on a metal item. The prosecutor generously allows you to have the tire iron tested at the local University using this new technology. A month later, you get the test results showing that the only DNA on the tire iron was that of an escaped prisoner wanted for two other homicides who was seen in the area where the killing occurred and near the time of Villow's death. Your client's DNA was not on the tire iron.

You want to file a Motion for New Trial since you are convinced that no jury would convict your client if presented with the DNA evidence.

48. What is the legal standard the trial court will use in vacating a conviction and granting a Motion for New Trial under Rule 33?

    (A) violation of defendant's substantial rights.

    (B) violation of defendant's constitutional rights.

    (C) if the interest of justice so requires.

    (D) if it appears beyond a reasonable doubt that the defendant was wrongly convicted.

49. Same facts as above. Assume you elect to file a Motion for New Trial for your client, Mr. Farlow. Which of the following is CORRECT under Rule 33?

    (A) you cannot file this motion because there has been more than 14 days since the jury verdict.

    (B) you must file this motion within one year of the jury verdict.

(C)   you must file within three years after the jury verdict.

(D)   you must file within 10 years after the jury verdict.

The Federal Rules of Criminal Procedure specifically allow three types of post-trial motions: Motion for Judgment of Acquittal (Rule 29), Motion for New Trial (Rule 33), and Motion in Arrest of Judgment (Rule 34).

50.   Compare the three motions on the basis of the grounds each recognizes as appropriate to reverse a conviction.

ANSWER:

Judge Weerde has just finished a trial involving over 100 witnesses and six months of court time. She has decided that this will not happen again in her courtroom. The duration of the trial required Judge Weerde to reschedule seven other trials originally set for the time taken by the unexpectedly long trial that just concluded.

She has now issued an order that no subpoenas will issue for court testimony without her written approval. Counsel seeking permission for a subpoena must convince Judge Weerde of an "extraordinary need" for the subpoena. You represent a defendant in a complex fraud case and you plan on issuing subpoenas for well over 50 people to establish that your client was not involved in the scam.

51. What arguments can you make against Judge Weerde's new rule requiring judicial permission for each trial subpoena?

ANSWER:

You are prosecuting a man for assaulting an elderly woman. Three days before trial, you receive an anonymous call giving the name of someone who allegedly witnessed the assault. You locate this new witness and want to subpoena him to testify for the government.

52. Under the Federal Rules of Criminal Procedure, who will actually issue this subpoena in the ordinary case?

    (A)   the presiding judge.

    (B)   the prosecuting attorney.

    (C)   the court clerk.

    (D)   any of the above.

You are defense counsel in a well-publicized federal bribery case. You have located a key witness who will provide strong evidence that your client knew nothing about the exchange of money underlying the prosecution. As far as you know, the prosecution does not know about this witness and you want to ensure that the witness surprises the prosecution at trial. You know that the prosecutor's office is located on the same floor as the clerk's office and that the prosecutor is close friends with many people who work in the court clerk's office. They often have lunch together and frequently go to a nearby bar after work. You want to subpoena this surprise witness but do not want the prosecutor to know you did.

53. Which of the following is the most sensible outcome under the Federal Rules of Criminal Procedure?

(A) in order to ensure anonymity, you, as defense lawyer, should not have a subpoena issued; rather you should simply ask the surprise witness to appear in court at a specific time to testify.

(B) you should have the witness subpoenaed but have the clerk's office keep the list of people subpoenaed in a sealed envelope locked in the office vault.

(C) you should not worry since the subpoenas are issued in blank and the clerk's office will not have a record of the names of people receiving a subpoena.

(D) you should ask the court to permit you to have the subpoena issued to "John Doe" so no one in the clerk's office will know who is subpoenaed.

United States District Judge Mohammed Al-Haftiri was presiding over a wire fraud case when, after the first week of a two-week trial, he developed severe appendicitis and had emergency surgery. He will be away from work for at least three months and possibly more.

The Chief Judge of the District Court, Judge Marilyn Foster, is looking at alternatives to complete the wire fraud case. The same day as the surgery, Judge Foster learned that her docket would be free for the next week because a scheduled trial was cancelled when the defendant entered a last-minute guilty plea.

54.   Under the Federal Rules of Criminal Procedure, what must the Chief Judge Foster do to assume responsibility over the wire fraud trial begun by Judge Al-Haftiri?

     (A)   secure the approval of all lawyers.

     (B)   secure approval of the defendant.

     (C)   simply certify that she is familiar with the record of the trial.

     (D)   Do nothing. Since Judge Foster did not hear the evidence presented in the first days of the trial, there must be a mistrial and the trial must be started all over before a judge who will hear all the proof.

Same facts as above, except Judge Al-Haftiri presided over the entire wire fraud trial but had emergency surgery two days after a guilty verdict was rendered and a month before a sentencing hearing was scheduled. Chief Judge Foster would like to complete the case by presiding personally over a sentencing hearing.

55.   Under Rule 25, Federal Rules of Criminal Procedure, what is the correct procedure?

     (A)   after a finding of guilt, another federal judge in that district may complete any tasks, including sentencing, because Judge Al-Haftiri is disabled and could not preside over the sentencing for the foreseeable future.

     (B)   the trial would have to be conducted again so a new judge could hear all the evidence and impose sentence.

     (C)   Judge Al-Haftiri, the only judge familiar with the case, would have to conduct the sentencing hearing when he recovers.

     (D)   the defendant has the choice of whether to delay the sentencing hearing until Judge Al-Haftiri returns or consent to a sentencing hearing presided over by another federal judge.

Your client was arrested for his third offense of drunk driving after being involved in a fatal collision that killed a family of three people, and their estate has filed a civil suit for wrongful death against your client. Your investigation showed that the prosecution in the criminal case will be able to prove that your client was very drunk at the time. Your client knows this. The drunk driving criminal case is scheduled to be tried well before the civil one. Your client has been reading law books and wonders whether a *nolo contendere* plea to the drunk driving case would make sense.

56. Advise your client.

ANSWER:

57. Under Federal Rule 11, what is one of the principle differences between a guilty plea and a no contest (or *nolo contendere*) plea?

(A) After the court has accepted a defendant's plea but before the sentencing, the defendant has a right to withdraw a *nolo contendere* plea without providing a reason but cannot withdraw a guilty plea without providing a fair and just reason.

(B) Before accepting a *nolo contendere* plea, the court is not required to determine voluntariness because it is presumed under the rule. However, the court must determine that a defendant who enters a guilty plea did so voluntarily and free of "force."

(C) The court is provided discretion in advising the defendant whether to seek a *nolo contendere* plea during plea negotiations, provided that the defendant's attorney is present. However, the court cannot be involved in a guilty plea negotiation.

(D) A *nolo contendere* plea is inadmissible in a subsequent criminal or civil trial where the defendant is involved. However, if the defendant enters a plea of guilty, that plea may well be admissible in a subsequent trial, assuming the other provisions of the Federal Rules of Evidence are satisfied.

Kimberly Killer was charged with first degree murder in a jurisdiction that has adopted the Federal Rules of Criminal Procedure. The prosecutor realized that a key witness is unwilling to testify. Without informing the defense attorney of this fact, the prosecutor made a formal offer that "if Kimberly would plead guilty to involuntary manslaughter, then Kimberly would serve no more than three years in prison." Kimberly immediately accepted the deal.

At the sentencing hearing, Kimberly told the judge that she pled guilty to involuntary manslaughter and admitted under oath that she committed the crime. The prosecutor told the judge about the three-year maximum sentence. The judge accepted Kimberly's plea, then vociferously condemned the prosecutor for downgrading the charge to involuntary manslaughter.

On the record the next day, the judge reconvened the parties and said that he had thought about the case and decided that he would not accept the involuntary manslaughter charge but would accept the plea to a charge of second degree murder. The judge then rejected the plea agreement limiting the sentence to a maximum of three years and took under advisement the sentence. The judge indicated that a five-year sentence and a 10-year probation "may well be appropriate in this case, but I need to think about it some more."

58.   What can happen at this point?

   (A)   Kimberly can withdraw the guilty plea and stand trial, but her admission of guilt regarding involuntary manslaughter is admissible at trial.

   (B)   Kimberly can withdraw the guilty plea and stand trial; her in-court admission of killing the victim is inadmissible at trial.

   (C)   The guilty plea has already been entered and the judge should sentence Kimberly to any sentence the judge thinks is appropriate, based on that authorized for involuntary manslaughter.

   (D)   Because of the doctrine of separation of powers, the plea agreement is between the prosecutor and the defendant; the trial court cannot reject a plea agreement that both sides knowingly and voluntarily decided was an acceptable resolution of the case.

David was an assistant to Governor Williams of the State of Jefferson. Federal authorities suspected the Governor was using campaign donations for his private purchases, in violation of federal election laws. David was aware of the Governor's misdeeds and helped hide some of them from auditors.

The Assistant U.S. Attorney entered a written deal with David that if David provided information and, if needed, "truthful trial testimony" leading to the conviction of the Governor, David could plead guilty to a minor felony and the government would recommend a sentence of no more than two years on probation. David's trial was postponed until after the Governor's trial, in which David testified and the Governor was convicted of all charges.

The federal prosecutor was dissatisfied with David's testimony in the Governor's trial, thinking that David's inability to remember some important transactions was a violation of the plea agreement. Accordingly, the prosecutor refused to recommend the probation sentence and said it took no position on the sentence David should receive. David's lawyer moved to enforce the initial plea agreement.

59.   What should the court do?

   (A)   conduct a hearing to determine whether David fully lived up to the bargain. If so, the deal must be honored and the prosecutor must make a good faith effort to request a sentence or no more than two years on probation or the court must so sentence David.

    (B)   deny the motion. Since the sentence had not been imposed, the prosecutor could change her mind at any time as long as it was done in good faith.

    (C)   the trial court has no authority to modify or interpret plea agreements; this is a function of the prosecutor because of separation of powers concerns.

    (D)   the prosecutor breached the letter and spirit of the plea agreement and the court should honor it by dismissing the charges against David, who should not have to relitigate a matter already resolved by the agreement.

60.   In *Brady v. United States*, 397 U.S. 742 (1970), the Supreme Court held that sentencing defendants who plead guilty to a lower sentence than those who are convicted after a trial:

    (A)   violates the Fifth Amendment by penalizing a defendant for asserting the right to a trial.

    (B)   is sufficiently coercive to make the plea involuntary.

    (C)   does not make the plea involuntary or unconstitutional.

    (D)   requires the court to sentence the defendant to the same sentence irrespective of whether there was a plea or a trial.

Sarah and Simone run a nice scam where they obtain stolen items from thieves and then sell the items on eBay, keeping 50% of the proceeds for themselves. One of their thief-clients is caught during a burglary and confesses to the police about how Sarah and Simone buy his stolen goods. Both are arrested. Sarah accepts a deal to plead guilty to knowingly receiving stolen property. The deal would entail a sentence of one year in prison and an agreement to testify against Simone, who has elected to go to trial. Sarah pleads guilty and receives the one-year sentence. She also testifies against Simone who, surprisingly, is acquitted. Apparently, the jury was not convinced that Sarah and Simone knew the items were stolen since each of their thief-clients claimed to have gotten the items legitimately (such as by gift, inheritance, purchased at a garage sale or flea market, or off Craigslist).

Sarah is unhappy with this result and moves the trial court to set side her prior guilty plea and allow her to go to trial.

61.   The court should:

    (A)   view Simone's acquittal as evidence that the charged offenses did not occur, a conclusion inconsistent with Sarah's guilty plea, and set aside Sarah's guilty plea since the two results are incompatible.

    (B)   set aside Sarah's plea under the doctrine of fundamental fairness.

    (C)   set aside Sarah's plea because Simone's acquittal sufficiently shows that Sarah's plea was not made voluntarily, knowingly, and intelligently since no one would enter the plea with such little proof of actual guilt, as established by the acquittal.

    (D)   enforce the plea agreement as written.

Jack was charged with several counts of child abuse and could have received a 30-year prison term. Jack disputed many of the less severe charges against him but, on the advice of counsel, agreed to plead guilty since there was substantial evidence of guilt and juries in the jurisdiction were notoriously unsympathetic to defendants in child abuse cases. Jack immediately directed his lawyer to negotiate a plea with the prosecutor to reduce the prison part of the sentence to the lowest felony punishment possible, regardless of the actual sentence.

Consistent with the plea agreement, Jack received a four-year prison sentence and was placed on probation. However, Jack's lawyer did not tell him about a new state law that rendered Jack ineligible to vote based on his felony conviction. Upon learning of this new law, Jack sought to have his guilty plea set aside and face a trial, even though if convicted he might receive a 30-year sentence. Jack's new lawyer argued that his first lawyer provided ineffective assistance by failing to advise Jack of all the consequences of pleading guilty.

62. How should the court rule in a jurisdiction that follows the Federal Rules of Criminal Procedure?

(A) Jack, as a citizen, is responsible for knowing about existing laws. His ignorance of this law is his own fault and will not invalidate his plea.

(B) The failure of Jack's lawyer to inform Jack about the post-release consequences would not serve as a basis for a successful ineffective assistance of counsel claim.

(C) The court is required to inform Jack of all the foreseeable consequences associated with pleading guilty. Since the court failed to inform Jack about these conditions, this constitutes reversible error and Jack should be allowed to withdraw his plea.

(D) Jack's lawyer had no responsibility to inform Jack of the new law.

Marilyn was caught while burglarizing a pharmacy in order to obtain drugs to satisfy her addiction. Her defense lawyer engaged in plea discussions with the prosecutor who agreed to recommend a sentence of no more than three years in prison on the condition that Marilyn agree to drug testing while in prison and for five years thereafter. The maximum authorized sentence was 10 years in prison. The prosecutor said the offer was good for 30 days.

Defense counsel knew from previous experiences with this prosecutor that the initial offer was simply a starting point for discussion and that the deal would get more favorable in later discussions. Counsel did not communicate this offer to Marilyn but planned on having serious discussions with her when better offers were made.

Because of a change in internal policies in the prosecutor's office, no better deal was ever made. The head prosecutor had decided it was time to get tough on drug store burglaries because there had been a 50% increase in them in the past year.

Six weeks later, plea discussions resumed. The prosecutor told defense counsel of the new emphasis and said the best offer now was a minimum of four years in prison with no drug testing required. Counsel told Marilyn of this offer and she accepted it rather than face a much more substantial sentence if she went to trial. She was sentenced in accordance with the deal, receiving a four-year sentence in prison.

Marilyn now wants to withdraw her plea and accept the earlier three-year plea that was never communicated to her. She argues that her Sixth Amendment right to effective assistance of counsel was violated.

63. How will the judge rule?

ANSWER:

Same facts as above, except defense counsel did communicate the three-year offer to Marilyn, told her about a likely more favorable offer in later negotiations, and counseled Marilyn to reject the offer, which she did. When the prosecutor's office changed policy after the first offer lapsed and the new offer was for four years instead of three, Marilyn opted to go to trial where she was convicted and sentenced to six years in prison. She now maintains that she was denied her Sixth Amendment right to the effective assistance of counsel by her lawyer's bad advice and that she should be allowed to accept the initial three-year sentence.

64. Which of the following is correct?

(A) Her claim will be denied because counsel, though wrong, did not perform below the standard of defense performance guaranteed by the Sixth Amendment.

(B) Her claim will be denied because she suffered no prejudice from her lawyer's advice since she got a fair trial, which is all she is entitled to have under the Sixth Amendment.

(C) Her claim will be successful because counsel is held to a very high standard of strict liability, meaning the advice must be correct.

(D) Her claim will be successful since the final result (a six-year sentence) is essentially twice the length of the one offered in exchange for a guilty plea.

Kenny is charged with felony assault for severely injuring a bouncer in a barroom brawl. A few weeks before trial, the junior prosecutor assigned the case offers Kenny a plea agreement where he will serve two years in prison. Kenny's lawyer is furious at this suggestion because the bouncer attacked Kenny, who merely defended himself.

Defense counsel goes directly to the head prosecutor to "talk sense." After a heated argument, the head prosecutor says, "You and your client are gonna pay for trying to go over the head of my assistant." The head prosecutor then reviews the charges against Kenny and discovers Kenny has several other felony convictions that could earn Kenny a mandatory life sentence under the state's "three strikes" law. Kenny is then charged under the three strikes provision, convicted, and given a life sentence. On appeal, Kenny's lawyer argues that the court should set aside the conviction based on prosecutorial vindictiveness, especially since the prosecution had originally offered only two years in prison.

65. How should the court rule?

(A) This fact pattern would shock the conscience of the court, which should overturn the felony conviction and sentence Kenny to two years in prison.

(B)   The court should overturn the sentence and allow the defendant an opportunity to accept the prosecutor's original offer of two years in prison.

(C)   The court should overturn the conviction. The prosecutor's conduct violates Kenny's right of equal protection and due process, since he is apparently the unfortunate victim of a quarrel between his lawyer and the prosecutor.

(D)   The court should uphold the conviction and the sentence. The prosecutor is ordinarily free to seek any charges allowed under the law.

Annette is arrested for embezzling from her employer. She maintains she is innocent because she always planned on returning the money. During plea negotiations, she agreed to plead guilty if the prosecutor would recommend no more than a two-year sentence. The prosecutor agrees. In court, Annette pleads to this deal. However, after doing some research and concluding she may well have a viable defense, Annette changes her mind and wants to withdraw her plea and have a jury trial.

66.   Under the Federal Rules of Criminal Procedure, which of the following is NOT correct?

(A)   If the court has not yet accepted Annette's plea, Annette may withdraw her plea for a "substantial reason that serves the interests of justice."

(B)   If the court has accepted her plea but has not yet imposed sentence, she may withdraw the plea if the judge rejects the plea agreement because the judge thinks the additional charges should not be dismissed.

(C)   If the court has accepted Annette's plea but has not yet imposed sentence, she may withdraw the plea if she can show a "fair and just reason for requesting the withdrawal."

(D)   If the court has accepted the plea and imposed sentence, Annette may not withdraw the guilty plea. She may only have it set aside on direct appeal or collateral attack.

You are defense counsel to a man who is charged with possession of a large amount of methamphetamine. Your client, however, has told you that the drugs were not really his, but rather belonged to his 18-year-old daughter, who has a promising professional career ahead of her, and that he is willing to plead guilty to protect her. The prosecution has offered a favorable deal of five years in prison as opposed to the 20-year sentence that could be imposed if the defendant were convicted in a trial. Your client asks if he can tell the judge at the plea hearing: "I plead guilty but I want you and everyone to know that the drugs were not mine."

67.   Is such a plea permissible under the Federal Rules of Criminal Procedure?

ANSWER:

Same facts as previous question. Your client adamantly refuses to confess to the drug possession charge but wants to accept the five-year offer. The problem is that the state has a statute providing that any person who pleads guilty must testify on the record, under oath, that he or she is in fact guilty of the crime and must also provide enough factual details to satisfy the court that the defendant really is guilty.

Since your client refuses to confess his guilt as required by statute, you filed a motion to allow him to plead guilty without the confession. At a motion hearing, you argue that the mandatory confession violates your client's Fifth Amendment protection against compelled self-incrimination.

68.   How should the court rule?

ANSWER:

Dora Holwell, a truck driver, is being prosecuted for the interstate transportation of stolen televisions. She wants to plead guilty and accept a favorable plea deal, but she also wants to tell the judge that she is really not guilty because she did not know the televisions were stolen. The judge's practice is to accept "best interests" or *Alford* pleas.

69.   What will be the effect of this plea?

   (A)   defendant is convicted but evidence of the conviction cannot be used against the defendant at a later civil trial since the defendant denied guilt.

   (B)   defendant is convicted but could withdraw her guilty plea at any time because she denied guilt in a timely manner.

   (C)   defendant is convicted.

   (D)   defendant is essentially offering a *nolo contendere* plea because she admits guilt and does not contest the charges in court.

Viktor Kote was believed to have abducted three small children. When Kote was captured, police believed that the victims possibly were still alive. Kote refused to answer any questions about the crimes. Frustrated and worried about the safety of the missing children, the local prosecutor said, "Kote, you'll only do 30 years for kidnapping if you will tell us where the kids are." Kote quickly said, "I accept your offer." He then directed police to a wooded hideout where all three child victims were found dead.

Outraged and facing growing community anger, the prosecutor indicted Kote for three counts of first degree murder and sought the death penalty. Kote's lawyer argued that a valid plea deal was in place and sued for specific performance of that deal. Prosecutors argued that Kote accepted the deal in bad faith, knowing the victims were dead.

70.   How should the court rule?

   (A)   the deal should be enforced as stated. Kote adhered to his part of the deal and the prosecutor must do so as well.

   (B)   the deal should be voided because of Kote's bad faith "acceptance."

   (C)   reject Kote's argument because there was no valid plea deal present.

   (D)   reject the deal since it was never accepted by the court. Until the court accepts it, either or both sides may withdraw from it.

The judges, prosecutors, and defense lawyers in a federal district met and agreed on a new "script" to use when defendants plead guilty in the local federal court. The script informs defendants of their rights and deals with other procedural matters. Rule 11 of the Federal Rules of Criminal Procedure applies.

71. Based solely on the limited facts above, which of the following is most accurate about cases handled using the new script?

    (A)   all the pleas entered using the new script are unconstitutional and invalid because the script was not the product of a federal statute.

    (B)   all the pleas entered using the script that was not approved by the Supreme Court are nevertheless valid under the harmless error doctrine.

    (C)   even though the script actually used was not formally adopted by the U.S. Supreme Court, it may still be a valid means by which to take a guilty plea.

    (D)   courts should not use a script. Rule 11 requires the court to read verbatim the pertinent parts of the rule so the accused is accurately apprised of its contents.

72. Which of the following rights, waived when a defendant pleads guilty, should NOT be on the list of those rights about which a judge under Rule 11 must inform the accused?

    (A)   jury trial.

    (B)   confrontation.

    (C)   effective assistance of counsel.

    (D)   self-incrimination.

You represent a professor of physics charged with producing weapons of mass destruction. Your client is an incredibly detailed and analytic person. She wants to know about the plea process since the prosecution has made an attractive offer. She asks you for a list of available pleas so she can carefully think through her options.

73. Under Rule 11 of the Federal Rules of Criminal Procedure, which of the following pleas is NOT specifically authorized?

    (A)   guilty plea.

    (B)   not guilty plea.

    (C)   *nolo contendere* plea.

    (D)   reserved plea.

Your client, Bert, high on cocaine, was arrested and immediately interrogated about two murders. He confessed to involvement in the killings.

Bert is charged with two counts of murder. The prosecution would surely use Bert's confession if the case goes to trial, but Bert was offered a deal in which he would receive a maximum of 30 years in prison for both homicides. Bert wants to take the deal but you believe there is a strong argument that Bert's confession is inadmissible because obtained while he was heavily drugged. Without the confession, the state's case is very weak and unlikely to result in a conviction.

74. Under the Federal Rules of Criminal Procedure, the best option for Bert is to:

(A) take the deal, plead guilty, and hope the appellate court will reverse because of the drugged confession.

(B) plead not guilty, then appeal the confession if he is convicted at trial.

(C) enter a conditional plea, reserving the right to appeal the confession issue.

(D) abandon the confession issue and take the favorable deal.

75. Same facts as above. If Bert does want to enter a conditional plea, which of the following is NOT true?

(A) the court must consent to the conditional plea.

(B) the government must consent to the conditional plea.

(C) the issue to be appealed must be so significant that any conviction would be reversed automatically if the appellate court agrees that the defendant's motion to exclude the evidence should have been sustained.

(D) the plea must include a written reservation so that the appellate court may be presented with a specific legal issue to resolve.

Judge Blumenthal is assigned administrative matters that include guilty plea proceedings under Rule 11.

76. When accepting a guilty plea under Rule 11, Judge Blumenthal must do all of the following EXCEPT:

(A) make sure defense counsel has thoroughly investigated the case before recommending that his or her client accept or reject any plea deal.

(B) ensure that the plea is voluntary.

(C) assure that there is a factual basis for the plea.

(D) inform the defendant of the maximum possible penalty, even if that penalty is greater than that to be recommended in the plea agreement.

An ambitious federal prosecutor has decided that guilty pleas result in sentences that are too low and therefore compromise deterrence. Accordingly, he has issued an order that bans all plea bargains and anything else that encourages pleas in the district. His goal is to go to trial whenever possible because defendants who are convicted after a trial receive longer sentences than those convicted after a plea.

77. Under Rule 11 of the Federal Rules of Criminal Procedure, which of the following procedures is possible only if the prosecutor consents?

(A) guilty plea.

(B) not guilty plea.

(C) conditional plea.

(D) *nolo contendere* plea.

Rule 11 of the Federal Rules of Criminal Procedure mandates that a judge accepting a guilty plea must inform the accused of the rights waived when entering a guilty plea.

78. Which rights must be noted as being waived if the accused pleads guilty?

ANSWER:

As an intern for the public defender's office, you assist defense attorneys in their representation of indigent clients, some of them having emotional and mental problems. One day, you accompany an attorney to interview a client who was just arrested for homicide. During the interview, the client described his recent trip to the moon where he encountered four sea monsters and he expressed great fear from the hundreds of "trapezoids" who are hiding under his cell bed.

Your boss has asked you and a co-clerk to prepare concise, informal memos on certain procedural issues concerning a possible insanity or mental disability defense. Your assignment is to assess whether Rule 12.2 of the Federal Rules of Criminal Procedure must be satisfied and, if so, what should be done. You are also asked to discuss briefly any benefits from using this Rule and any consequences if the rule is not followed. Your co-clerk will research all other issues.

79. Draft a short memo responding to your boss's concerns.

ANSWER:

You are an Assistant United States Attorney handling the case of William Coke, the head of the largest drug distribution ring in town. Coke has been charged with murder for the September 17th drive-by shooting off Kathy Rivalle, head of the second largest drug ring who had expressed a strong intent to take over all drug sales in the area. During plea negotiations, defense counsel told you that Coke was nowhere near the location of the shooting when it occurred. He was in a town 200 miles away visiting a cousin.

You believe that Coke is the shooter and that the cousin, and perhaps other as yet unknown witnesses, will lie in order to help Coke avoid a conviction. In order to best defend against Coke's likely alibi defense, you want to make sure you follow all procedures mandated by Rule 12.1 of the Federal Rules of Criminal Procedure.

80. Which of the following is NOT necessary if the government wants formal notice of Coke's intended alibi defense and alibi witnesses so it can prove the alibi is unsubstantiated in fact?

(A) the government must request in writing that the defense notify the government of an intent to present an alibi defense.

(B) the government's request must also notify the defense of the time, date, and place of the alleged homicide.

(C) the government must notify the defense of the name, address, and telephone number of each witness the government intends to rely on to establish the defendant's presence at the homicide.

(D) the government must disclose to the defense its investigative file showing every contact it made in order to find witnesses to rebut the alibi defense.

81. Same facts as above. If Coke's attorney does want to offer an alibi, which of the following does defense counsel NOT have to do under Rule 12.1 (assuming the government complies fully with this rule)?

(A) provide an affidavit from the defendant who swears under oath, subject to perjury, that the alibi defense is offered in good faith.

(B) provide the prosecutor with notice of an intent to offer an alibi defense.

(C) provide the prosecutor with the location where the defendant claims to have been at the time of the homicide.

(D) provide the prosecutor with the names, addresses, and telephone numbers of all alibi witnesses the defendant intends to call.

Rules 12.1 and 12.2 of the Federal Rules of Criminal Procedure are notice rules that share some common features but have significant differences as well. Read the following features that *could possibly* be shared by both:

I. Aimed at preventing trial surprises.

II. Triggered by the government/prosecution.

III. Requires disclosure of the names and addresses of all persons the government and the defense contacted to see if they would support or not support the alibi or insanity defense.

IV. If required notice is ultimately withdrawn, the withdrawn notice cannot be introduced as evidence in a later trial against the party who withdrew the notice.

82. Which of the above are common characteristics of both Rule 12.1 on alibi defense and Rule 12.2 on insanity defense?

(A) only (I) and (II).

(B) only (I) and (IV).

(C) only (III) and (IV).

(D) none is a characteristic of both rules.

You are a law clerk to a trial judge in a jurisdiction that follows the Federal Rules of Criminal Procedure. Your boss has noticed that many lawyers are sloppy with some of the notice rules.

83. Your assignment is to prepare a short memo about the consequences of not following the notice Rules 12.1 and 12.2.

ANSWER:

Jeremy was convicted of rape 11 years ago. He has maintained since his arrest that he is innocent and does not know who committed the crime. The assault victim had struggled with her assailant and had actually scratched him so hard that minute pieces of skin were found under her fingernails. Unfortunately, the amounts of measureable DNA were too small for DNA testing at the time.

Recently a local university announced it had developed a DNA test that could extract DNA from a sample the size of the head of a needle. Jeremy wants his case reopened and the substance found under the victim's fingernails analyzed using the new DNA test. He is convinced it will show he was not the rapist.

You represent Jeremy and learn that the police department no longer has the material found under the rape victim's fingernails. Department policy required the destruction of all evidence 10 years after a conviction became final. You file a motion to overturn Jeremy's conviction based on the destruction of the possibly exculpatory evidence.

84.   Under the United States Constitution, the conviction will:

   (A)   be reversed since the police were responsible for not destroying evidence that might have exonerated Jeremy.

   (B)   be reversed because the police have a duty to preserve all relevant evidence in a serious case.

   (C)   be upheld since it is unclear whether the destroyed evidence would have helped or harmed Jeremy's case.

   (D)   be upheld unless Jeremy can demonstrate that the police acted in bad faith in destroying the evidence.

You are a prosecutor preparing for a trial next month involving Marvin Green, an accountant charged with embezzling from the aerospace company for whom he worked. During plea negotiations, defense counsel has claimed that her client is innocent and that someone else "set up" Mr. Green to hide the real culprit.

As you review the file, you find a document that you had not noticed before. The item is one sheet of unsigned, undated paper bearing the handwritten words: "Green is innocent. He is being framed by the man who took the money." You ask around and no one in your office and no police officer involved in the investigation knows anything about the document. You do not plan to introduce the item into evidence. Even if it helped you prove guilt (which it does not), you believe it is inadmissible hearsay.

The defense made a formal request under Rule 16 for all documents in the government's possession that are material to the defense.

85. Must you turn this item over to the defense? Why or why not?

ANSWER:

You are the defense lawyer for Sybyl Richards, charged with being head of a large drug conspiracy. The federal government had investigated her for two years and last week indicted her for a number of crimes, including four counts of conspiracy to murder. You want maximum discovery to help you prepare for a very challenging trial. You plan on using all possible discovery approaches and you have carefully reviewed the possibilities.

86. Under Rule 16 of the Federal Rules of Criminal Procedure, all of the following material must be turned over to the defendant upon request EXCEPT:

(A) defendant's oral statements to the police before and after arrest in response to interrogation if the government intends to use the statement at trial.

(B) defendant's prior criminal record.

(C) any internal government record in connection with investigating the case against the defendant.

(D) any record of examination of the defendant's physical or mental condition that the government intends to use at trial.

87. Which of the following does the government NOT have to turn over to the defense pursuant to Rule 16?

(A) a written statement the defendant gave to the police, which is now in a prosecutor's case file.

(B) the substance of an oral statement the main government witness gave to the police.

(C) a copy of the defendant's criminal record, which is in the prosecutor's case file.

(D) written business documents, now in the government's possession, from the company that sold bullets to the accused a few days before the murder was to occur and showing all sales for five days before the homicide.

Same facts as above. Your review of discovery under the Federal Rules of Criminal Procedure has revealed that Rule 16 of the Federal Rules of Criminal Procedure generally requires reciprocal discovery. Your goal is to get as much information as possible from the government while disclosing as little as possible to the government.

The general protocol of Rule 16 is that the defense requests certain information from the prosecution, which the prosecution is then obligated to give the defense. This triggers a reciprocal duty by the defense to disclose similar information to the prosecution. However, not all information is subject to this reciprocity requirement.

88. Which of the following is NOT subject to this reciprocity requirement?

QUESTIONS & ANSWERS: CRIMINAL PROCEDURE — PROSECUTION AND ADJUDICATION

    (A) written or recorded statement of defendant.

    (B) reports of examinations and tests.

    (C) documents and tangible objects.

    (D) summary of testimony of expert witness intended to be used at trial.

Same facts as above. You realize you need to look even closer at Rule 16 since you have a good deal of material that you simply cannot turn over to the government without seriously compromising your client's position.

89.   Which of the following statements is ACCURATE under Rule 16 with regard to defense counsel?

    (A) You must give the prosecution access to all documents not protected by the work product rule that are material to the prosecution's trial preparation.

    (B) You must turn over anything, other than the defendant's statements, that is helpful to the prosecution just as the prosecution must turn over materials helpful to the defense under *Brady v. Maryland.*

    (C) You must give the government access to reports of mental examinations of the defendant if you have the reports in your file and intend to use them in your case-in-chief at trial.

    (D) Because of the Fifth Amendment's self-incrimination clause, the defense does not have to disclose anything that would tend to incriminate the client, Sybyl Richards.

Same facts as above. You are concerned that the extensive electronic and hard copy materials possibly shedding light on this very complex case involving Richards could lead one or even both sides to violate the extensive disclosure required by Rule 16.

90.   Which is NOT a remedy specifically authorized by Rule 16 for failure to comply with this rule's requirements?

    (A) in extreme and rare situations, if the violation was a significant and intentional one by the defense counsel, grant a prosecution motion to convict for all charges.

    (B) grant a continuance.

    (C) prohibit the party from introducing any undisclosed evidence.

    (D) enter any just order.

Same facts as above. You realize that discovery in federal criminal cases places certain burdens on each side. Failure to comply with a responsibility can lead to sanctions. As you formulate the approach you will take during the upcoming trial, you want to make sure you abide by your discovery responsibilities and the government by its. Your review of all the pertinent parts of the Federal Rules of Criminal Procedure shows that certain procedures must be initiated by the government.

91. Which of the following processes is begun by an action of the *prosecution*?

(A) notice of insanity defense.

(B) notice of intent to use expert testimony on mental condition.

(C) notice of alibi.

(D) notice of defense based upon public authority.

Same facts as above. You know if you were defending your client Richards in a civil case you would likely take many depositions to learn about the available evidence. You think a deposition in this criminal case could be very helpful since there are many possible witnesses, including undercover law enforcement agents, and you need to know their likely testimony in order to prepare fully for the lengthy trial ahead.

92. If you want to use a deposition, taken in the United States, under Rule 15 of the Federal Rules of Criminal Procedure, which of the following is NOT accurate?

(A) the deposition may be taken only in "exceptional circumstances" and in the "interest of justice."

(B) because of security concerns, the defendant has no right to be present at the taking of the deposition but has a right to be present in court when the deposition is entered into evidence.

(C) the deposition can be taken only with the court's permission.

(D) the deposition may be used at trial under the Federal Rules of Evidence.

93. Same facts as above. You think a series of depositions would greatly speed up your investigation and are considering filing a motion requesting 35 depositions to "assist in preparing the defense." Under Rule 15, assess the likely success of this motion.

ANSWER:

Same facts as above. Your investigator has learned that a key prosecution witness, Micky Fell, has been detained by the government to ensure that he will appear at your client's trial scheduled to begin in a month. Fell was a middleman who bought drugs from your client then had his group of 20 young men and women sell them in assigned areas throughout town.

You also learn that Fell is represented by Tovah Greenblatt, a well-respected criminal defense lawyer and former Assistant U.S. Attorney, who has been instructed by her client to do whatever she can to have Fell released from detention. Apparently, Fell is convinced that his life is in danger in jail because he is a government informant who will soon testify against Richards. Lawyer Greenblatt has suggested that Fell be deposed under Rule 15(a)(2), Federal Rules of Criminal Procedure, and then released from jail.

94. If this material witness is to be deposed, which of the following is accurate?

(A) the witness may make a formal written motion to be deposed.

(B) the witness must sign under oath the deposition transcript before being released.

(C) the witness may be discharged after being deposed.

(D) all of above.

Same facts as above. As you investigate the cases against your client Richards and begin to prepare for trial, you realize that the indictment is very fuzzy in some respects. Your preparation would be better if you knew more precisely exactly what facts the government is alleging.

95. Using the Federal Rules of Criminal Procedure, which of the following is most likely to help you find out more about the charges which are stated in general language in the indictment?

(A) bill of particulars.

(B) request for admission of facts.

(C) interrogatories.

(D) deposition.

Federal Rule of Criminal Procedure 26.2, often called the *Jencks* Rule, requires disclosure of a witness's statement after the witness has testified on direct examination in a federal criminal case. The purpose of this procedure is to facilitate cross-examination.

96. While Rule 26.2 applies to many federal proceedings, in which of the following is it inapplicable?

(A) sentencing hearing.

(B) preliminary hearing.

(C) suppression hearing.

(D) grand jury proceeding.

Judge Martinez is presiding over a murder trial. The prosecution alleges that the case involved a drive-by shooting motivated by a failed drug operation. Margaret Spotter, who was cleaning her window at the time of the shooting and saw it occur, testified on direct examination for the prosecution that the defendant was the lone gunman. A year ago, shortly after the incident, Ms. Spotter provided the police with a written statement containing significant detail about the event and the shooter. The prosecutor has Ms. Spotter's statement in her file.

97. Under Federal Rules of Criminal Procedure 26.2, which of the following reasons would support Judge Martinez's decision NOT to order the prosecutor to provide the defense with a copy of this statement to use in its cross-examination of Ms. Spotter?

(A) the statement is in the prosecution's case file that was prepared for the sole purpose of assisting the prosecutor to get ready for trial, hence it is protected by the work product rule.

(B) the defense made no motion requesting this statement.

(C) the statement would not help the accused since it simply supported what Spotter said on direct examination.

(D) Ms. Spotter strongly opposes allowing the defendant to see her statement.

You are defense counsel in a criminal case involving large-scale money-laundering. You have made a thorough investigation of the matter and plan on using only two witnesses since you think the government may be unable to meet its burden of proof beyond a reasonable doubt once all the witnesses testify. Your witnesses are your client's accountant and your client. There is no accountant-client privilege in your jurisdiction.

To assist you in preparing for the examination and cross examination of your two witnesses, you have taken extensive written statements from each. Some of these statements contain information about other illegal activity unknown to the government. Frankly, you do not want to turn over any such statements to the government, as required by Rule 26.2, after each of your two witnesses testifies.

98. Must you comply with Rule 26.2 for both witnesses?

ANSWER:

Oliver "Killer" Thompson is head of the Biker Boys motorcycle gang. He was indicted for 37 counts of federal crimes, including extortion, conspiracy to murder, drug trafficking, aggravated assault, and arson. Much evidence for the indictments was the product of reports by an F.B.I undercover agent who infiltrated the gang for almost two years. The agent, code named Intrepid, had supplied details that were used in the search and arrest warrants for Thompson and have led to evidence and witnesses that will be used at the trial.

The defense has filed a Motion to Reveal Identity of Informant. Defense counsel argues that she needs this information in order to challenge the search and arrest warrants and to prepare for trial. As lead prosecutor, you do not want to reveal the identity of your informant who is still functioning undercover with the gang and whose life would definitely be in danger if his or her identity were revealed. You do not plan on calling (or even mentioning) this agent at trial.

99. How do you think the trial court will rule on this motion and why?

ANSWER:

Allison and Jennifer conspired to manufacture and sell methamphetamine. They made the meth in a trailer in Albert County, bagged it for sale in Baker County, and sold it in Carroll and Dover Counties. All four counties are in the State of Bankston.

They were arrested when one of their street sellers was arrested in Dover County and told the police about Allison and Jennifer in exchange for a lenient sentence. Manufacturing and selling meth is a crime in all four of the specified counties as well as under federal law.

100. Under the usual state jurisdiction and venue rules and under Rule 18 of the Federal Rules of Criminal Procedure, which of the following would have jurisdiction to try them for possessing and transporting the drugs?

    (A) the United States District Court in the federal district that covered Dover County.

    (B) the Dover County criminal court.

    (C) the Albert County criminal court.

    (D) all of above.

Donald kidnapped Reginald Farnsworth IV, the six-year-old son of one of the richest men on earth. He planned on ransoming the child for several million dollars. Donald snatched Reginald from a school yard in the State of Truman, and then drove across state lines to a remote cabin in the State of Roosevelt, where he used his cell phone to communicate his demands to Farnsworth's father. The police traced Donald's cell phone and arrested him at the cabin.

101. Where is the proper jurisdiction (Truman or Roosevelt or both) to try Donald for kidnapping and why?

ANSWER:

Rules 20 and 21 of the Federal Rules of Criminal Procedure specifically authorize a motion requesting a change of venue for certain purposes.

102. Which of the following is NOT true with regard to such a motion?

    (A) the defendant may file the motion to transfer for trial in order to obtain a fair and impartial trial.

    (B) the government may file the motion to transfer for trial to obtain a more convenient venue; the defendant's consent is unnecessary.

(C) the defendant may move to transfer for plea and sentencing.

(D) The United States Attorneys in both locales must approve in writing any transfer for plea and sentence.

Defendant Herman, who is in a wheelchair, is being tried for negligent homicide. Since the federal courthouse where the trial is scheduled has extremely poor facilities for the disabled, Herman wants to transfer the trial to another federal district in the same state. There, the modern courthouse is fully accessible and is only two blocks from Herman's home. The defense counsel now seeks a change venue under Rule 21 of the Federal Rules of Criminal Procedure.

103. For a transfer of trial, which of the following is NOT required under Rule 21?

(A) the consent of the government.

(B) a motion by the defendant.

(C) the motion must ordinarily be initiated before arraignment.

(D) the consent of the court.

104. Under the Federal Rules of Criminal Procedure's provisions for joinder and severance, which of the following statements is TRUE?

   (A) offenses that may be joined together in an indictment may be joined together for trial.

   (B) offenses may be joined for indictment but may not be joined for trial since the criteria are different for indictments and trial.

   (C) offenders may be joined for trial but offenses may not be so joined because of the danger that evidence about one offense would be used improperly to find guilt for others.

   (D) offenses may be joined in an indictment and trial only if they all occurred at the same time.

You are the Hazzard County prosecutor in the State of Duke, which follows the Federal Rules of Criminal Procedure. Sheriff Cletus Coaltrain informs you that he has just arrested Cooter, a local mechanic, for various felonies and misdemeanors. Since your office is very busy, you would like to have as few trials as the law allows. Ignore any perceived venue problems.

Cooter has been charged with the following crimes:

   I. Conspiracy with several customers in Hazzard to commit theft by disguising minor automotive damage so that it would appear to insurance investigators that the vehicle was a total loss.

   II. Illegal dumping of hazardous waste products generated routinely during auto repairs. This is a misdemeanor in the State of Duke punishable up to six months in prison.

   III. Conspiracy to commit insurance fraud by teaching other mechanics how to disguise motor vehicle damage so it would seem a wrecked car is a total loss and then splitting the proceeds of the scam with the other mechanics.

105. Which of the above crimes can be joined together at a single trial of Cooter under Rule 8(a) of the Federal Rules of Criminal Procedure?

   (A) None of the above; each must be tried separately.

   (B) I and II.

   (C) I and III.

   (D) II and III.

After a massive manhunt covering three states, Philip Brown was arrested and charged with murdering and dismembering five prostitutes in State X. As far as the authorities can determine, Brown picked up each victim as she walked the streets in search of clients, took the victim to a remote area, then stabbed and strangled her to death. Three of the five bodies were seriously decomposed; some had been on the ground for over a year and were reduced to bones. All were found in the same four-acre forest. The exact cause of death for some of the victims could not be identified, though the two most recent had definitely been strangled and stabbed. Brown confessed to three of the homicides but denied knowing anything about the two other deaths. A week later he retracted the confession and claimed he had been coerced by police to give it. The judge has ruled that the confession is admissible but defense counsel may still argue that it had been coerced and should not be given any weight by the jury.

The prosecution charged all five homicides in one indictment with five counts of first degree murder. Brown's defense attorney has filed a timely motion under Rule 14 of the Federal Rules of Criminal Procedure to have each homicide tried in a separate proceeding.

106. You are the judge's law clerk. Your boss has indicated that she is inclined to grant the defendant's motion and has asked you for reasons that she can put into her opinion to justify her ruling granting the severance. Briefly state your reasons to the judge. Do not draft a formal memorandum.

ANSWER:

Raj was arrested after a traffic stop in a national park when the arresting officer saw a pistol on the floor of Raj's car. No one else was in the car. Raj was immediately searched and a baggie of heroin was found in his pocket. He was charged with two crimes: possession of heroin and being a felon in possession of a firearm.

107. If the U.S. Attorney wants to join these offenses in one *trial* under Rules 8(a) and 13, would they survive a Rule 8 motion to sever for improper joinder?

(A) Yes. The heroin and the gun were found at the same time and the two crimes are closely interrelated since drug dealers often carry weapons to protect themselves and their valuable drugs.

(B) Yes. In order to preserve resources, prosecutors can join all charges they have against one defendant in the same trial.

(C) No. Gun possession is an entirely different kind of crime from drug possession. The two are not the same or similar character or part of a common scheme or plan.

(D) No. It would be unfairly prejudicial to include the gun possession count and the drug count in the same trial.

Laura Weisz is the Mayor of Battleford, a large town in a jurisdiction that has adopted the Federal Rules of Criminal Procedure in all relevant aspects. When businesses sought contracts to do various projects for the City of Battleford, Weisz — successfully — dropped hints that a business may be "lucky" if Weisz were given "a token of appreciation." One such crime involved an envelope with $15,000 in it, given by the President of the Sewer Excavating Company. Over a period of two years,

Mayor Weisz received cash, free trips to resorts, a new car, a boat, jewelry, and an expensive golf club membership.

Paul Dykstra was Director of Purchasing for the City of Battleford. Like his close friend, Mayor Weisz, Dykstra encouraged "a bit of love" from people wanting to do business with the City. He, too, received many "gifts" from potential contractors. One friendly gesture was an envelope filled with cash from the Sewer Excavating Company, which eventually was given the City contract despite not submitting the lowest bid.

The federal prosecutor has charged both Weisz and Dykstra with accepting a bribe from the Sewer Excavating Company and not reporting this income to the Internal Revenue Service. The Weisz charge was based on the envelope containing $15,000 cash. The Dykstra charge was for the cash-filled envelope.

108. Which of the following, if true, would be most helpful to the prosecutor if he or she tries to join Weisz and Dykstra in one trial under Rules 8(b) and 13?

    (A) an eyewitness saw Weisz and Dykstra at a restaurant and overheard Weisz say, "Do you think we can get any more for the sewer deal or are they tapped out?"

    (B) Weisz and Dykstra were both spoken to by potential contractors wanting to work on the sewer modernization project.

    (C) when Mayor Weisz was arrested for bribery, Dykstra put up the money for her bail bond.

    (D) Weisz's method of collecting the "gifts" mirrored Dykstra's in every way.

You are a criminal defense lawyer representing a lawyer charged with stealing client funds from the firm's trust account. Your client, with a spotless record and reputation, always planned on repaying the money as soon as a large inheritance from his deceased father cleared probate.

Unfortunately, your client was joined for trial with Ronald Silva, the law firm's bookkeeper and your client's lover. You discover that Silva has a criminal conviction for embezzlement and is a heavy drug user widely known to be willing to lie to get money. Much of this information may well be admissible against Silva at the joint trial. You fear that the jury will hold your client at fault for associating with Silva. This is an especially grave concern because of the personal relationship between your client and Silva.

109. What standard will you have to meet in order to persuade the trial court to grant a Rule 14 motion for discretionary severance?

    (A) The government has the burden to show that joinder is not prejudicial to either defendant's rights. It must establish by clear and convincing evidence that there was no serious risk of actual prejudice to a specified trial right or likelihood that a jury would be unable to make a reliable decision.

    (B) The government has the burden to show that joinder is not prejudicial to either defendant's rights. The government must establish by a preponderance of evidence that there was no reasonable possibility of prejudice, or of a reasonable uncertainty that a jury might not be able to make a reliable decision.

(C) Your client has the burden to show prejudice. Most courts require that he show a serious or substantial risk that a joint trial would compromise a specific trial right or would prevent the jury from making a reliable judgment of guilt or innocence.

(D) Your client has the burden to show prejudice. He must show a reasonable possibility of prejudice from the joint trial.

Debbi Duncan, a radical anti-industrialist, was charged in federal court with mailing a series of six deadly pipe bombs to factories throughout the Midwest. The bombs were sent every two months. Three of the bombs exploded when opened. Investigators believe that Debbi was in the process of mailing the bombs to a series of locations that, when plotted on a U.S. map, would make the pattern of a $ sign. Six bombs were mailed before federal agents arrested Debbi. The U.S. Attorney has sought to try her on all six bombings in one trial.

110. Which of the following facts, if true, would most strongly support Debbi's Rule 8(a) Motion for Relief from Improper Joinder of Offenses?

(A) since each bomb was sent to a factory a long distance from the target of any other bomb, it would be virtually impossible for the defense to adequately investigate each location in time for one trial, resulting in a trial that was unfairly prejudicial to the defense with its limited resources.

(B) each bomb was mailed from a different Florida post office.

(C) each bomb was manufactured differently and had a different kind of detonation device.

(D) only three of the bombs actually exploded. Regarding the three bombs that did not explode, the federal grand jury only returned misdemeanor charges on those occurrences and it would be unfair to join felonies and misdemeanors in the same trial.

Duncan v. Louisiana, 391 U.S. 145 (1968), is a seminal case in Sixth Amendment jury trial law.

111. What is the primary rationale for *Duncan v. Louisiana's* ruling that a defendant charged with a serious offense has the right to a jury trial?

(A) to increase accuracy in fact-finding.

(B) to increase public respect for verdicts by multiplying the number of persons deliberating on each case.

(C) to provide a defense against arbitrary law enforcement by including the public in the decision-making process.

(D) to give members of the public insight into the justice system.

A defendant was charged with a single count of violating federal laws that prohibit hunting and fishing in protected wildlife sanctuaries. The punishment is as follows:

> (b) Punishment — The punishment for an offense under this section is a fine of not more than $10,000, imprisonment for not more than six months, or both.

> (c) Mandatory Restitution — Upon conviction under this section, the court shall order restitution in an amount equal to value of the wildlife illegally killed or harmed seriously.

The trial judge rejected the defendant's timely request for a jury trial and convicted him after a short bench trial. He was sentenced to serve six months in prison and fined $700. The defendant appeals, claiming that his Sixth Amendment right to a jury trial was violated.

112. You are the appellate judge in this case. On the basis of the United States Constitution, how do you respond to the defendant's appeal?

ANSWER:

113. In which case below would the defendant be entitled by the Sixth Amendment of the United States Constitution to a trial by jury?

(A) a 17-year-old defendant in juvenile court facing a charge carrying a maximum sentence of five years in a juvenile detention facility.

(B) a 22-year-old defendant in adult criminal court facing a charge carrying a maximum sentence of six months in prison and a $750 fine.

(C) a 14-year-old defendant in adult criminal court facing a charge carrying a maximum sentence of nine months in prison.

(D) a 9-year-old defendant in juvenile court facing a charge carrying a maximum sentence of five years in a juvenile detention facility.

You are a prosecutor planning an important trial that has attracted much pretrial publicity since it involved a family that had a long involvement in gang-related crimes in the area. You will need as many peremptory challenges as you can get, so you would like to have potential jurors you do not want on the final jury to be excluded by the judge for cause. This will preserve your peremptory challenges for jurors potentially biased by the extensive media coverage. You have just found out that one potential juror was married to another potential juror.

114. Do you think the court will excuse both potential jurors for cause?

ANSWER:

115. In jury selection in a capital case, which of the following is NOT correct?

(A) the judge may exclude a potential juror for cause only when it is "unmistakably clear" that the juror "would automatically vote against imposition of capital punishment without regard to any evidence that might be developed at the trial of the case."

(B) the judge may exclude for cause any juror whose views "would prevent or substantially impair the performance" of the juror's duties as a juror in accordance with the court's instructions and the juror's oath.

(C) the judge may exclude any juror who could not impose the death penalty because of strong religious beliefs.

(D) all of above are correct statements of death penalty law.

You represent a defendant charged with embezzling money from the Dark Cross Church, a small splinter denomination of the Baptist Church. During jury selection, you learn that one member of the Dark Cross Church is on the jury panel that has been tentatively seated, subject to the parties' exercise of their peremptory challenges. You would like to use a peremptory challenge to exclude the juror because you are concerned she will be biased against the defendant who is charged with embezzling from her church.

116. May you use a peremptory challenge to exclude the potential juror for this reason?

ANSWER:

You are a federal prosecutor in a case where you think a jury would be sympathetic to your position. Unfortunately for you, defense counsel has figured out the same thing and wants a bench trial.

117. Which of the following reasons is INCORRECT regarding waiver of a jury trial under Rule 23 of the Federal Rules of Criminal Procedure?

(A) defendant's waiver of a jury must be in writing.

(B) the court must approve any such waiver.

(C) the government must consent to any such waiver.

(D) the government may not block any such waiver because the Constitution gives the defendant the right to have or not to have a jury trial.

Donald Deff is facing trial for robbery. The state's case is overwhelming since the robbery was recorded on two security cameras that clearly showed Deff as the culprit.

Under state law, the jury in such cases will consist of nine jurors. Deff wants a jury of 12. After being convicted of all charges, Deff appeals, claiming that the trial violated his Sixth and Fourteenth Amendment rights to a jury of 12 persons and requesting a retrial in front of a 12-member jury.

118. You are the appellate judge. How do you respond?

(A) the appeal is denied because a nine-member jury is constitutionally permissible.

(B) the appeal is denied because while a 12-member jury is constitutionally required, the use of a nine-member jury in this case is harmless error because the overwhelming proof of guilt meant that Deff would have been convicted by a larger jury, anyway.

(C) the appeal is granted because everyone tried in an American court has a constitutional right to a jury trial, and the definition of a jury when the Sixth Amendment was adopted was a body of 12 members.

(D) the appeal is successful since Deff's constitutional right to a jury trial was violated by the jury of nine members. Such a verdict may not be the result of careful deliberation, consistently achieved by a group of people representative of the community at large.

Catherine Drinke was charged with driving under the influence, a crime punishable under state law as a misdemeanor by a year in prison. To save money, a year ago the state legislature adopted a criminal procedure rule approving a five-member jury to be used in all misdemeanor jury trials, including drunk driving. Defendant Drinke's motion for a 12-member jury was denied, and she was subsequently convicted as charged. On appeal, she claims that the trial by a five-person jury violated her Sixth and Fourteenth Amendment rights to a jury trial.

119. You are the appellate judge. How do you respond?

(A) the appeal is denied because a five-member jury is constitutionally permissible for this crime.

(B) the appeal is granted because Drinke's constitutional right to a jury trial for this crime was violated using a five-member jury. Such a verdict may not be the result of careful deliberation, consistently achieved by a group of people representative of the community at large.

(C)   the appeal is denied because, while a 12-member jury is the proper size, the mistake was harmless error since Drinke confessed to consuming a six-pack of beer shortly before the arrest, flunked a field sobriety test, and then a blood test showed her to have a very high blood-alcohol content.

(D)   the appeal is granted, because Drinke has a constitutional right to a jury trial, and the definition of a jury when the Sixth Amendment was written was a body of 12 members.

You are a member of a state legislative committee investigating how to increase the efficiency in the state judicial system, which is suffering from an extensive backlog of pending criminal cases. The committee chair has suggested that a real problem is that a state statute mandates that jury verdicts be unanimous in criminal cases. If the jurors are not unanimous, there is a "hung jury" and the case may be retried, taking up scarce judicial resources for a second trial in the same case. The chair has asked your opinion on the lawfulness and wisdom of changing state law to permit a jury verdict of 10-2 to convict or acquit.

120.   What is your opinion regarding the non-unanimous jury verdict?

ANSWER:

Daisy Defendant was tried and convicted for murder in Delta County. An ethnic group that is a minority nationwide and forbids its members from participating in elections makes up 60% of the citizens and residents in Delta County. Since the list of registered voters forms the entire jury pool, persons of this ethnicity make up only 10% of the jury pool. The entire jury venire of 500 persons from which Daisy's 12-person petit jury was ultimately selected included 2% of the ethnic group and the 12-member petit jury that convicted Daisy contained only one jury member who belonged to the ethnic group. Daisy's conviction has been attacked on the basis of this statistical disparity.

121.   Acting under authority of the United States Constitution, how should a court dispose of this attack on Daisy's conviction?

(A)   Daisy's conviction should be affirmed, because there is no constitutional guarantee of statistical representation of the community in the jury selection process.

(B)   Daisy should be retried, because the composition of the petit jury violated Daisy's right to be tried by a petit jury representative of the community in which the crime was committed.

(C)   Daisy should be retried, because the composition of the jury pool and venire violated her right to be tried by a petit jury selected by a process that does not systematically exclude a segment of the community in which the crime was committed.

(D)   Daisy's conviction should be affirmed, because the disproportionate composition of the jury pool, venire, and petite jury constitute a violation of the civil rights of members of the severely underrepresented ethnic group; it does not violate any of Daisy's rights.

DEFENDANT'S RIGHT TO ATTEND TRIAL AND RELATED PROCEEDINGS

You were appointed to represent a man charged with insurance fraud. Trial starts in five minutes and your client, released on bail, has not appeared yet. He was supposed to meet you outside the courthouse an hour ago.

122. You check Rule 43, Federal Rules of Criminal Procedure to assess the possible consequences if your client does not show up in a few minutes. Under this rule, which of the following is CORRECT?

   (A) the trial may proceed in the defendant's absence if the defendant had attended all pretrial conferences and hearings, agreed to the trial date, but failed to appear for the start of trial.

   (B) the trial may proceed if the defendant attended all pretrial conferences and hearings, appeared for the first day of trial, and then disappeared after the government presented a very persuasive case to the jury.

   (C) the trial may proceed since the defendant's absence before trial began constitutes a valid waiver of the right to attend the trial.

   (D) the trial may proceed if defense counsel agrees in open court to waive the accused's presence.

123. The defendant's right to attend generally does NOT apply to:

   (A) jury selection.

   (B) the entire trial.

   (C) announcement of the verdict.

   (D) argument in appellate court.

Upyars Mann was on trial for burglary for breaking into an Army Reserve building and destroying over $20,000 worth of equipment. Mann was a member of War Never, a pacifist group protesting the very existence of an army. During the trial, Mann became upset with a key government witness, Col. Janet Adams, who, as commander of this installation, testified (in full uniform) about the break-in and the items damaged in it.

Mann interrupted Col. Adams many times, shouting obscenities at her. The judge warned Mann several times, even threatened to hold him in contempt. Mann persisted, now also yelling at the judge and threatening to "take care of" both the "fascist" Col. Adams and the "lackey" judge.

The judge gave Mann a final warning that Mann would be removed from the courtroom if he did not behave. When Mann continued to disrupt the trial, the judge had Mann forcibly removed from the courtroom and taken to jail. After 90 minutes, the judge halted the trial, had Mann returned to the courtroom, and told Mann he could remain if he promised to behave. Each time Mann told the judge to "go to hell." Mann was then removed again and returned to jail for another 90 minutes. He ended up being absent for the rest of the trial.

After the closing arguments, the defense moved for a mistrial because Mann had been denied his constitutional right to be present at his own trial. You are the judge's clerk.

124. What advice will you give the judge on the motion for a mistrial?

ANSWER:

The United States Supreme Court has recognized that a judge presiding in a case where the defendant is persistently disruptive has a number of available options.

125. Which of the following is NOT one of them, according to the leading case of *Illinois v. Allen*, 397 U.S. 337 (1970)?

(A) find the defendant in contempt of court.

(B) remove the defendant from the courtroom.

(C) bind and gag the defendant.

(D) instruct the jury that it may consider the defendant's courtroom behavior when it assesses guilt or innocence.

Daniel Defendant was tried for the brutal murder of several elderly persons. The trial in a small courtroom was highly publicized, and many members of the press and general public wished to attend the trial. Once the courtroom seats were all filled, the bailiffs began turning people away, explaining that the courtroom was full and that fire codes prohibited the admission of any more people. Among those turned away were some members of the press, some members of Daniel's family, two members of the victims' families, and others who just wanted to observe. Throughout the trial, as people would leave the courtroom, a corresponding number of people were allowed in to take their places. Daniel has appealed his conviction, arguing that his Sixth Amendment right to a public trial was violated since many members of the public were barred from the courtroom.

126. How should the appellate court respond to Daniel's appeal?

ANSWER:

You are a law clerk to a newly appointed judge who has asked you to research when the courtroom may be closed to the public. You review many cases and have advised your judge that generally the courtroom may not be closed to the public, though a narrowly focused closure may be appropriate in some situations.

127. Which of the following is NOT a legitimate reason for a judge to order that an appropriately narrow portion of court proceedings be closed to the public?

    (A)　protecting all minor victims of sexual assault from intimidation and embarrassment.

    (B)　protecting a witness or party from grave physical harm or protecting the welfare of a particular crime victim.

    (C)　protecting national security matters that would be compromised by public hearings.

    (D)　protecting the identity of an undercover agent whose life could be compromised if the public and press were apprised of the agent's identity.

Polly Popularity is on trial for a crime that the popular press has been decrying for some time. Not wanting his every decision and ruling to be picked apart and analyzed, the judge has ordered that the trial be closed to the public and the press. Polly has not objected because she thinks a closed trial may benefit her.

The major area newspaper, however, has filed a suit against the trial judge, seeking an injunction against the trial closing. The paper makes two arguments. First, the paper maintains that closing the trial violates Polly's Sixth Amendment right to a public trial. Second, the press argues that closing the trial violates the First Amendment guarantees of freedom of the press and freedom of assembly.

128. Which, if any, of these is/are valid ground(s) for the newspaper's demand for an injunction?

(A) the judge's order violates the First Amendment.

(B) the judge's order violates the Sixth Amendment.

(C) the judge's order violates the First and Sixth Amendments.

(D) none of the newspaper's arguments is valid.

You represent Charles Berner charged with arson of an elementary school. The fire was set at 2:00 p.m. on a week day when children were present. Fortunately, all the children escaped unharmed. Six children were scheduled to testify. Two of them actually saw your client set the fire in a trash can in a hallway.

The judge hearing the case closed the courtroom to non-family members of the child-witnesses during the testimony of all the child witnesses. The judge feared the children would be intimidated by the crowd and the menacing glare of your client. Your client was convicted of all charges. You are considering an appeal based on a violation of your client's Sixth Amendment right to a public trial.

129. Which of the following could cause your appeal to fail?

(A) You cannot prove any prejudice from the closure.

(B) There may have been harmless error since the proof against your client was very strong.

(C) You did not object to the closure.

(D) Some members of the public (the family members) were permitted to attend at all times.

Harry Darwin is on trial for marijuana possession. He has been convicted on the same charge eight times in the past six years, and the same judge has presided over all of those cases. Darwin has waived a jury and the judge is conducting the bench trial for the current allegations. In an effort to speed up the trial, the judge tells defense counsel that although Harry wants to testify, he "doesn't need to testify. I have heard him testify many times. He is going to say the drugs weren't his. So, unless you tell me this is not what he will say, I will assume that is what he will say now and so his testimony is unnecessary. I rule he cannot testify because it would be cumulative evidence." The defense counsel objected. Darwin was convicted of all charges.

130. You are handling the appeal for the defense lawyer. Does a criminal defendant have a constitutional right to testify at the defendant's own trial? If so, what is the constitutional basis for the right?

ANSWER:

Quinn Quiet is on trial and chose not to testify. In closing argument, the prosecutor plans to argue to the jury that the reason Quinn did not testify and deny any of the evidence was because Quinn knew he would be committing perjury if did deny them. The judge anticipates the prosecutor may make such an argument, so she has planned to give the jury the following instruction:

> Every defendant has the constitutional right to testify or to not testify. If a defendant should choose not to testify, that decision does not give rise to any interference or presumption against the defendant or about the facts in the case. Such a decision to remain silent should never be considered in determining that defendant's guilt or innocence.

In an unrelated case, Tammy Talkie decided to testify on her own behalf. That prosecutor plans to tell the jurors that they should consider the reliability of the witnesses testifying. Specifically, he plans to argue that the jury should evaluate Tammy's credibility because she, unlike all of the State's witnesses, was able to remain in the court and listen to all of the other testimony before testifying in the case.

131. Which, if any, of these statements would violate the respective defendant's right not to testify under the United States Constitution?

   (A) the prosecutor's closing argument in *State v. Quiet* would be unconstitutional.

   (B) the judge's planned jury instruction in *State v. Quiet* would be unconstitutional.

   (C) the prosecutor's comments in *State v. Talkie* would be unconstitutional.

   (D) none of the statements discussed above would be unconstitutional.

Tina Triggerhappy, on trial for second degree murder, has claimed self-defense. While the events leading to the shooting were hotly disputed, the prosecution and defense witnesses all testified that Tina placed a gun in direct contact with Vinnie Victim's head and pulled the trigger three times, fatally shooting Vinnie.

After the close of proof, the district attorney filed Proposed Jury Instruction #1, which reads in part:

> Should you find that the State has proven beyond a reasonable doubt every element of the charge of second degree murder, you may nevertheless acquit Tina if you find that she has proven by a preponderance of the evidence the following elements of the defense of self-defense. The statutory elements of self-defense are then listed. Self-defense is an affirmative defense in the jurisdiction and the burden is on the defense to prove self-defense by a preponderance of the evidence.

The district attorney also filed Proposed Jury Instruction #2, which states, "A person is conclusively presumed to intend the natural and probable consequences of his or her acts." Tina's attorney objected to Proposed Instructions #1 and #2, claiming that both of them unconstitutionally place the burden of proof on Tina.

Afraid that the judge might deny Proposed Jury Instruction #2, the district attorney has filed Proposed Jury Instruction #3 as an alternative. Proposed Jury Instruction #3 reads, "Should you find the following facts to be true: (a) that Tina aimed a loaded gun at a living person, and (b) that Tina then pulled the trigger of that loaded gun, then you may infer that Tina intended to kill." Tina's attorney has lodged the same objection to Proposed Instruction #3.

132. Assuming that the three jury instructions accurately apply the relevant state law, which of the proposed jury instructions violates the United States Constitution?

   (A) proposed Jury Instruction #1 unconstitutionally shifts the state's burden of proof.

   (B) proposed Jury Instruction #2 unconstitutionally shifts the state's burden of proof.

   (C) proposed Jury Instruction #3 unconstitutionally shifts the state's burden of proof.

   (D) all of the proposed jury instructions — #1, #2, and #3 — unconstitutionally shift the state's burden of proof.

You are chair of a legislative subcommittee making recommendations on improving the insanity defense in your state. Two issues being addressed are: (1) which side should have the burden of persuasion and (2) what should the standard of proof be to establish the insanity defense.

133. Which of the following options would be permissible under the United States Constitution?

(A) placing the burden of persuasion on the government to prove the defendant was sane beyond a reasonable doubt.

(B) placing the burden of persuasion on the defendant to prove the defendant was insane by a preponderance of the evidence.

(C) all of above are constitutional.

(D) none of above is constitutional.

Ibn Al-Aqqad is a new federal prosecutor about to prosecute his first trial. Defense counsel just filed a motion allowing the defense to offer the last closing argument. Counsel argued that the opportunity to have the final word with the jury is essential since the defendant's liberty is at stake. The court denied the motion and has decided to follow Rule 29.1 and the usual rules concerning closing argument.

134. Assuming Al-Aqqad wants to take full advantage of the chance to address the jurors under Rule 29.1, when will he face them to make an argument after all the proof has been presented?

   (A) only before defense counsel makes her closing argument.

   (B) before and after defense counsel makes her closing argument.

   (C) only after defense counsel makes her closing argument.

   (D) after the jury returns to the courtroom with questions that arose during deliberations.

Felix is charged with a very complicated swindle involving forged esoteric bank obligations. The prosecution offered two expert witnesses to explain the forged documents and how they resulted in huge profits for Felix. After researching the law, defense counsel wants the jury instructed that it should accept expert testimony with caution. There is some weak support for this instruction.

135. Under Federal Rule of Criminal Procedure 30, what should defense counsel do to present the request to Judge Huang?

ANSWER:

136. When must Judge Huang rule on defense counsel's request under Rule 30 of the Federal Rules of Criminal Procedure?

    (A) as soon as possible to give both lawyers time to adjust to the instructions.

    (B) after the prosecution rests and before the defense presents its case.

    (C) before the closing statements.

    (D) after the closing statements.

Judge Huang has informed defense counsel that he will not give the requested jury instruction because the instruction was not required by existing law and would confuse the jury. Defense counsel wants to object to this ruling and preserve the issue for appellate reversal. His research has located several cases from other jurisdictions indicating that the requested instruction is permissible.

137. What must defense counsel do to preserve the issue for appellate consideration?

ANSWER:

138. In criminal cases, a SPECIAL VERDICT (sometimes called special interrogatories):

(A) is reserved for capital cases where the jury must make specific findings about aggravating and mitigating circumstances.

(B) requires the jury to answer specific questions in which it resolves facts required for elements of a crime or sentence.

(C) is permissible only if requested by the defendant.

(D) violates due process.

John and Jerry needed money to fuel their expensive cocaine addictions. They solved their money problems by robbing the Superbank. Both entered the bank at the same time with drawn guns, took money from a terrified teller, and left together. They were arrested within an hour, both confessed, and both were identified by all four eyewitnesses in the bank. Bank security cameras clearly showed the robbery and the faces of both John and Jerry. When plea negotiations broke down, they had a joint trial. Shocking everyone (including John and Jerry), the jury convicted them both of bank robbery but acquitted them of conspiracy to rob the bank.

139. Because proof against them for both robbery and conspiracy to rob was so strong, these verdicts are inconsistent verdicts and:

(A) at least one must be overturned since John and Jerry were so clearly guilty of both the conspiracy and bank robbery.

(B) both verdicts must be overturned and a new trial ordered because the verdicts were inconsistent with one another and with the proof.

(C) both verdicts must be overturned because the jury did not follow the court's instructions with regard to resolving the elements of each crime.

(D) both verdicts will stand.

140. Which of the following is TRUE about jury nullification in most locales?

(A) A potential juror may not be excused from jury service because he or she claimed the right to follow or not follow the law in reaching a verdict as long as the juror promised to act on his or her sincere belief.

(B) Because of the ancient lineage of jury nullification, the jury must be told of this inherent power under the Due Process Clause.

(C) Judges do not give a jury instruction on the jury's power to nullify in order to serve justice, irrespective of the evidence.

(D) Defense counsel must be permitted to argue for jury nullification since a jury has the power to do so.

You represent Bryan Tucker, charged with killing two people during a convenience store robbery. The main issue during trial is whether Tucker was insane at the time of the crime. Both sides present well-credentialed mental health expert witnesses.

So far, jury deliberations have been going on for three days. The foreperson just sent the trial judge a note saying, "I don't think we are going to be able to decide this case. Strong opinions for and against insanity. Unlikely to change anyone's mind. What should we do?"

The jurisdiction permitted the judge to use an *Allen* charge in appropriate cases.

141. What is an "*Allen* charge" and when should it be used?

ANSWER:

142. The *Allen* charge has engendered a great deal of criticism. The primary argument against its use is:

(A) it coerces the minority into agreeing with the majority.

(B) it coerces the majority into agreeing with the minority.

(C) it is unfair to the prosecution because it leads to more defense verdicts.

(D) it produces too many hung juries.

Five Years Ago. On July 1st, five years ago, Larry Kidd decided he needed lots of money so he could retire from his job as a street seller of methamphetamine. He formed a plan to kidnap Margaret Childe, the only daughter of a Silicon Valley billionaire.

Kidd kidnapped Childe on August 1st of that year in Grainger County in broad daylight as Childe walked home from school. Three people on the street observed the kidnapping, gave the police a detailed description of the kidnapper and the green getaway van used. One even memorized most of the numbers and letters of the van's license tag.

Kidd immediately demanded ransom. Childe's father paid Kidd $10 million, but Childe was never found and Kidd was not apprehended immediately.

Four Years Ago. Four years ago, after intensive investigation by several law enforcement agencies, Kidd was indicted for kidnapping on February 1 by the Grainger County Grand Jury. An arrest warrant was issued that same day.

Three Years Ago. Kidd was arrested in Mexico on April 1st living under an assumed name, and immediately brought back to the United States, where he was taken before a federal judge for an initial appearance. All three of the eyewitnesses to the kidnapping selected Kidd from a lineup, he fit the description each eyewitness gave of the kidnapper, and his green van also matched the crime vehicle and had a license tag that included the numbers and letters remembered by the eyewitness.

Trial was scheduled for October 1st of that year, but on September 1st, Kidd fired his appointed lawyer and hired you to represent him. That day you filed a Motion for a Continuance to give you ample time to prepare for trial. Your client maintains he was hiking in the woods alone 20 miles away when the kidnapping occurred. The prosecutor did not object and the court granted a continuance until February 15th the next year.

Two Years Ago. The rescheduled trial (set for February 15th) two years ago was postponed again when the government filed a last-minute Motion for a Continuance because one of the three eyewitnesses was missing. You vigorously opposed the continuance and demanded a speedy trial, but the trial judge again postponed the trial until later in the year.

Both sides filed a total of six more successful continuance motions over the next 18 months. Reasons given included the head prosecutor (the only government lawyer completely familiar with the case) unexpectedly gave birth to a daughter almost a month earlier than scheduled (you demanded a speedy trial and opposed this continuance since the assistant prosecutor on the case was familiar with the case and could represent the government); the judge became ill (and granted a continuance without consulting with either side); you needed more time to locate a new possible alibi witness; you had another trial that was scheduled to begin the same day as a rescheduled one for Kidd; there was a bomb scare that closed the courthouse for the day trial was to begin; and the courtroom assigned for the trial was needed for another trial that lasted far longer than anyone had predicted.

One year Ago. The trial was eventually held on August 1st a year ago. The alibi witness you had located the year before unexpectedly died from a drug overdose a month before the August 1st trial.

This witness, who was a drug addict, had been camping in the woods the day of the kidnapping and thinks he "might" have seen Kidd walking there at that time, but could not be sure since it was a long time ago and he was high on drugs at the time. Kidd was convicted of all charges and given a life sentence.

143. You are the defense lawyer representing defendant Kidd on appeal. Discuss the approach you should take to assert that his constitutional speedy trial right was violated by the extensive delay.

ANSWER:

Defendant Duane Simpson is serving a 10-year sentence in the State of Boerum for armed robbery. Under state law he is ineligible for parole and will have to serve the entire 10-year term. Now after serving three months of the sentence, Simpson's lawyer informed him that he was just indicted in the State of Brooke for murdering his girlfriend, who was mysteriously found dead in her home six months ago, well before Simpson entered prison.

Simpson maintains that he was playing poker in the back room of a bar when the homicide occurred, but is concerned that he will be unable to locate and obtain the trial testimony of three alibi witnesses if the State of Brooke's trial is not held until he is released from prison in almost 10 years.

144. Under the Sixth Amendment's speedy trial guarantee, which is correct?

(A) Simpson has no right to have his homicide trial in the State of Brooke held until he can appear in person in that state in about 10 years.

(B) Simpson has no right to have his trial held in the State of Brooke because the speedy trial guarantee does not apply to prisoners lawfully incarcerated in another jurisdiction.

(C) Simpson has a Sixth Amendment right to have, upon his demand, the State of Brooke authorities make a diligent effort to bring him to trial in that state.

(D) Simpson has a Sixth Amendment right to have, upon his demand, a prompt trial in the State of Boerum (where he is incarcerated) on the outstanding homicide indictment issued in the State of Brooke.

Your client Carla was arrested a week ago and charged with use of the mails to defraud four investors in a Ponzi scheme. You think your client would benefit from a speedy trial that would not allow the government enough time to find and sort through the thousands of documents involved in the alleged fraudulent scheme. You want to know of any time limits imposed by the Federal Speedy Trial Act of 1974.

145. Under the Federal Speedy Trial Act of 1974, the indictment ordinarily must be issued within how many days after Carla's arrest?

(A) 10 days.

(B) 30 days.

(C) 60 days.

(D) One year.

Assume that your client Carla, described in the previous question, is indicted 28 days after her arrest and you are eager to proceed to trial. However, you have advised your client that you want to take the maximum time under the Federal Speedy Trial Act of 1974, but do not want to request a continuance. The additional time will permit you to investigate this case thoroughly, have your experts carefully examine many pertinent documents, and let you negotiate a possible favorable deal with the prosecutor handling the case.

146. Under the federal Speedy Trial Act, when must trial be held, absent acceptable reasons for a delay?

(A) within one year of arrest.

(B) within 70 days of the indictment.

(C) within one year of the indictment.

(D) within two years of completion of the crime.

147. Comparing the ordinary time permitted between indictment and trial under the Sixth Amendment's speedy trial guarantee and the Federal Speedy Trial Act, which of the following is correct?

(A) The time limits for the two are identical.

(B) Trial under the constitutional speedy trial guarantee will likely be faster.

(C) Trial under the Federal Speedy Trial Act will likely be faster.

(D) The constitutional speedy trial is inapplicable since it assesses the time between the crime and indictment, not between indictment and trial.

Mary Linda was indicted for manufacturing methamphetamine in her barn. When the federal judge handling this case was promoted to the Court of Appeals, the judge for whom you clerk was assigned the case as the newest federal district judge in the District. Your judge has carefully reviewed the file and found the following events had occurred:

(1) The defense filed a motion that the government responded to after 60 days;

(2) The defense took an interlocutory appeal that was rejected by the appellate court four months later;

(3) Defense counsel sought and gained the court's approval to conduct a mental examination of Mary Linda to determine whether she is fit to stand trial. The examination took 14 days to complete;

(4) The government obtained another 30 days of extension because the government's evidentiary documents were misplaced in its office.

148. As instructed by your judge, you have researched the federal statute and found that of the above delays, all of them are to be excluded from calculating the time deadline for trial under the Federal Speedy Trial Act of 1974, EXCEPT:

(A)   the 60 days it took the government to respond to the defense motion.

(B)   the four months needed to resolve an interlocutory appeal.

(C)   the 14 days it took to determine whether Mary Linda is mentally fit to stand trial.

(D)   the 30 days it took for the government to locate the missing evidence.

The national media has launched an extensive campaign criticizing federal judges for being inefficient and lazy, resulting in extensive trial delays in many cases. A newly seated federal district judge in your area is rumored to have aspirations for higher judicial positions. It has been reported that a newly appointed federal judge has decided to establish a "rocket docket" in which a trial would be held within 15 days of indictment, except in extraordinary circumstances when the judge would grant a continuance motion.

You are President of the local chapter of Criminal Defense Lawyers for Justice, which at its last meeting unanimously condemned the new time limits as making it virtually impossible for defense counsel to prepare thoroughly for trial. The members authorized you to research the issue and present the chapter's position to the new judge. You first look into whether due process or the Federal Speedy Trial Act places any limits on scheduling cases too quickly.

149. What will you find?

ANSWER:

Donald committed a burglary on October 1, 2011. He was arrested on April 1, 2013, indicted July 1, 2013, and eventually tried on November 1, 2014.

Defense counsel is exploring whether the applicable three-year statute of limitations has run so that the case must be dismissed.

150. When does the "clock begin to run" for the three-year statute of limitation in Donald's case?

(A) on October 1, 2011, when the burglary occurred.

(B) on April 1, 2013, when he was arrested.

(C) on July 1, 2013, when he was indicted.

(D) on November 1, 2014, when the trial began.

151. Same facts as above. When does the statute of limitations ordinarily stop running, assuming only the following occurs?

(A) When the defendant is indicted.

(B) When the defendant pleads not guilty and asks for trial.

(C) When the trial begins.

(D) When the court announces judgment after the jury verdict.

The concept of "tolling" is important in assessing whether the statute of limitations has been violated in a particular case.

152. What does it mean that the statute of limitations is "tolled?"

(A) the statute has been exceeded.

(B) the statute has started to run.

(C) the running of the statute of limitations has temporarily stopped.

(D) the initial event starting the running of the statute of limitations has not yet occurred.

You are a newly appointed judge and are reviewing the files of cases you are scheduled to hear in the next month. Several include unresolved motions to dismiss because of double jeopardy. You realize you know little about double jeopardy but wonder exactly what the Double Jeopardy Clause says.

153. What is the proper language of the Fifth Amendment double jeopardy provision?

    (A) "No person shall be convicted twice."

    (B) No person shall "be subject for the same offense to be twice put in jeopardy of life or limb."

    (C) No person shall "be subjected to double jeopardy."

    (D) No person shall "be tried more than one time for the same crime."

The United States Supreme Court has routinely held that the Double Jeopardy Clause applies to three separate constitutional protections.

154. Which of the following is NOT barred by double jeopardy?

    (A) second prosecution for the same offense after an acquittal.

    (B) second prosecution for the same offense after a conviction.

    (C) second prosecution for the same offense after a mistrial based on a hung jury.

    (D) multiple punishments for the same offense.

A jury in an insurance fraud case acquitted the defendant who allegedly submitted a false request to an insurance company for reimbursement for $75,000 worth of jewelry allegedly stolen from her home. The jury acquitted despite strong prosecution evidence, including a confession.

The prosecutor talked with several of the jurors and was troubled by several matters. The government then filed a Motion to Set a New Trial Date Because of Jury Errors. Defense counsel filed a response arguing that a new trial was barred by the Double Jeopardy Clause because of the acquittal.

155. Which of the following would bar a retrial because of double jeopardy?

    (A) the jury acquitted because it misunderstood the jury instructions and erroneously thought the government had to prove that the insurance company paid the claim with the knowledge that it was fraudulent.

(B) the jury acquitted with four jurors bribed to vote to acquit.

(C) both of above would bar a retrial.

(D) none of above would bar a retrial.

156. Which of the following would permit a retrial following a decision by a trial judge to acquit for insufficient evidence?

(A) the judge granted the acquittal because of a misunderstanding of the elements that the government must prove beyond a reasonable doubt.

(B) the judge granted the acquittal because the judge had erroneously excluded the government's key evidence.

(C) the judge granted the acquittal, took a break, and then reversed the acquittal decision upon further reflection.

(D) none of above permits a retrial.

Defense counsel Lionel Washington and Judge Kelly O'Reilly have had a long and unpleasant history. It is well known that they despise one another, but Judge O'Reilly is the only judge now presiding over criminal cases in the jurisdiction where Washington has a thriving criminal defense practice. The other judge with criminal jurisdiction is quite ill and has taken an extensive leave from the bench.

During a hotly-contested criminal trial over responsibility for a cache of drugs found in an attic of a house shared by two defendants, Washington, representing one of the two defendants, had lost a series of important objections to government evidence. He and the judge had traded insults which grew in intensity and viciousness. After one such loss, Washington said in open court, "Judge, perhaps next time I make an objection I will use shorter words, less complicated sentences, and speak slower."

Judge O'Reilly became visibly furious. He immediately banged the gavel and said loudly, "This case is over. The jury is dismissed. Mistrial." He then stormed out of the courtroom.

The prosecution immediately filed a Motion for a New Trial Date in order to start the trial again. Defense counsel Washington filed a Motion to Prevent Further Proceedings Because of the Double Jeopardy Clause.

157. What result on these motions?

ANSWER:

Same facts as above, but assume that, immediately after the outburst about using shorter words, defense counsel Washington said to Judge O'Reilly, "Judge, things seem to have gotten out of hand and the jury has seen it all. I ask for a mistrial so we can start fresh with a jury untainted by this unpleasantness." The real reason for the request was that the defense case had been going poorly and Washington hoped that he would fare better with a second shot at an acquittal.

158. What result on the two motions (government's motion to set a new trial date and

defendant's motion to oppose a new trial because of double jeopardy concerns)?

ANSWER:

Erik was charged with transporting illegal firearms across state lines, a federal crime, and was acquitted in a jury trial. Disappointed by the verdict, the Assistant U.S. Attorney (AUSA) looked over the case file and the applicable statutes. She found that 18 U.S.C. § 922 prohibits an alien from possessing a firearm and Erik is in the United States as a registered alien. Before she goes any further, the AUSA consults case law on double jeopardy.

159. Under the *Blockburger* approach to double jeopardy, which of the following is the correct test to determine whether transporting firearms across state lines and "alien in possession of a firearm" are the "same offense?"

(A) are there some common elements in the two crimes?

(B) does each crime require proof of a fact that the other does not?

(C) did the legislature intend for someone to be tried in a separate proceeding for both crimes?

(D) did the two offenses occur during the same transaction or set of acts?

Edmund Jamison was charged with physically striking Valery Victim two times on January 1st last year. The first incident occurred at 1:00 a.m. and the second an hour later. Jamison was tried for the first assault and was acquitted. Defense counsel has filed a motion to dismiss the second prosecution because collateral estoppel, applicable as part of the double jeopardy guarantee, bars the additional proceeding.

160. How should the court rule on the motion to dismiss?

ANSWER:

Boris Ignatov was arrested with 10 pounds of methamphetamine. He was charged with (1) manufacturing methamphetamine and (2) trafficking methamphetamine, and convicted of both in a short trial. Judge Lange sentenced Ignatov to consecutive sentences totaling 17 years (10 years for manufacturing, seven years for trafficking). Ignatov's lawyer has filed a Motion to Bar Second Sentence Given in Violation of the Double Jeopardy Clause.

161. What result?

(A) Ignatov cannot be convicted or sentenced for the two charges since the crimes occurred at the same moment in time.

(B) Ignatov cannot be sentenced for the two crimes because they both require the offender to have possession of methamphetamine.

(C) Ignatov can be sentenced for the two crimes if the legislature enacted separate sentences for these offenses and intended for both of them to be imposed on the same offender.

(D) Ignatov can be sentenced for the two crimes since, under *Blockburger*, they are not the "same offense."

Terrence Scott was convicted of arson and sentenced to five years in prison. Several months prior to this conviction, Scott was indicted for another arson. While in prison for the first arson, Scott pled guilty to the second arson and was sentenced to another three years, to be served upon completion of the five-year sentence for the first arson.

A year later the appellate court, acting on Scott's appeal, reversed the first arson conviction because illegally seized evidence had been used by the government, and ordered a new trial for the first arson. Scott was then retried for the first arson, convicted, and given a 10-year sentence. The trial judge specifically announced that the 10-year sentence was based, in part, on the fact that Scott had also been convicted of the second arson. Scott now wants to challenge the 10-year sentence as violating the Double Jeopardy Clause.

162. A harsher sentence after retrial in a case is:

(A) illegal because double jeopardy bars a harsher sentence on retrial.

(B) illegal because equal protection bars a harsher sentence on retrial.

(C) possible since any sentenced authorized by state sentencing law is permitted if the defendant chooses to appeal a conviction and a new trial is ordered; the appeal is a waiver of double jeopardy protection.

(D) possible if events, such as the defendant's second conviction after the first trial, justified the increased penalty.

Judge Matthews selected a jury in a capital case involving a hired assassin. Just before the new jury was sworn, Judge Matthews collapsed in the courtroom and died on the way to the hospital. The autopsy revealed he had been poisoned but there was no evidence of who administered the deadly drug. The chief judge immediately took over the case, dismissed the jury, and set a new trial date before another judge.

Defense counsel filed a Motion to Dismiss Because of Double Jeopardy to prevent the second trial. The prosecution's response argued that jeopardy had not attached and the second trial was permissible.

163. When does jeopardy attach in a jury trial?

(A) when jury selection formally begins.

(B) immediately after the indictment is issued and signed.

(C) when the jury is selected and sworn.

(D) when the first witness is sworn.

Changing the facts, what if the capital defendant had waived a jury and opted for a bench trial.

164. When does jeopardy attach at a bench trial?

    (A) when the defense gives its closing argument.

    (B) when the prosecution rests its case in chief.

    (C) when the court has heard all the evidence.

    (D) when the first witness is sworn.

Justin Liu successfully represented a defendant on appeal from a conviction for intentional odometer tampering with intent to defraud. Defendant owned a used car lot and had sold a car which had an odometer that showed only 106,000 miles when it should have shown 206,000 miles.

The appellate court overturned the conviction. The government has now filed papers to retry the case. Liu is exploring possible avenues to prevent the retrial.

165. Which of the following grounds for the appellate reversal would bar the retrial because of double jeopardy concerns?

    (A) the trial court erroneously suppressed important defense evidence.

    (B) the weight of the evidence was insufficient to convince the appellate court of guilt.

    (C) the trial judge gave an incorrect jury instruction on how the deadlocked jury should continue deliberating on the case.

    (D) there was not sufficient evidence of guilt presented at the trial.

Errin Heade grew marijuana on her porch deck and sold it just about anywhere she went. On May 5th, she harvested pot in Chicago (her home) and then sold it in Wisconsin. She was accompanied by her cousin but the cousin later got mad at Heade and told everything to a Chicago detective. Assume that trafficking in marijuana is illegal under federal law as well as in Wisconsin, Illinois, and Chicago (under local ordinance). Heade's defense lawyer is concerned that his client could face marijuana possession charges in four jurisdictions (U.S., Illinois, Wisconsin, and Chicago) for the incident of harvesting and selling the pot on May 5th.

166. Which of the following sets of places could NOT prosecute Heade for the marijuana trafficking on May 5th without violating the Double Jeopardy Clause?

    (A) United States and Illinois.

    (B) Illinois and Wisconsin.

    (C) United States and Chicago.

    (D) Illinois and Chicago.

In 1972, the Supreme Court of the United States held that the death penalty as applied violated the Eighth Amendment. *See Furman v. Georgia*, 408 U.S. 238 (1972).

167. The Court invalidated the death penalty because:

    (A)   the death penalty was racially biased.

    (B)   the death penalty was a violation of international law.

    (C)   the method of execution was cruel and unusual punishment.

    (D)   the death penalty was arbitrarily and capriciously imposed.

The Supreme Court of the United States has limited who is eligible for the death penalty.

168. Which of the following populations MAY BE executed under the Supreme Court cases?

    (A)   people who were under age 18 when they killed.

    (B)   people who have significantly sub-average intellectual function.

    (C)   people who are incompetent at time of proposed execution.

    (D)   people who while engaged in commission of a dangerous felony unintentionally kill an individual.

The Supreme Court has also limited the types of criminal involvement that may be the subject of the death penalty.

169. Which of the following would be a valid crime for a state to sanction by the penalty of death?

    (A)   rape of an adult woman.

    (B)   rape of a child.

    (C)   minor participation in a murder where the offender had a reckless indifference to human life.

    (D)   major participation in a murder where the offender had a reckless indifference to human life.

    (E)   all of above.

You were appointed to represent Leland Ferrell charged with the intentional homicide of the dean of his college and facing the death penalty under state law. Your investigation has revealed that Ferrell was sexually assaulted by a priest when he was a young boy and your psychiatrist expert is prepared to testify that your client is "especially prone to violence against authority figures" because of the incident.

Your client was convicted of first degree murder and you are now in the sentencing phase. You call your psychiatrist as a witness. The prosecutor objects, arguing that the testimony is inadmissible "because in our jurisdiction we have aggravating and mitigating factors. Our legislature has limited the mitigating factors to six topics and your psychiatrist would not address any of them." The judge has asked for your response.

170. What argument should you make?

ANSWER:

171. Which of the following is TRUE about procedures in capital cases?

(A) a state is free to have a judge make findings about the existence of aggravating circumstances and then make the death penalty decision, as long as the judge carefully follows state laws on death penalty procedures.

(B) a state may impose a mandatory death penalty for a killing involving torture of a child under age ten.

(C) a state may allow victim impact statements to be introduced in a capital sentencing hearing because it provides a human face to the prosecution's case.

(D) all of above are true.

172. Of the four traditional theories of punishment (retribution, deterrence, rehabilitation, and incapacitation), which is/are NOT designed to decrease future criminal activity?

   (A) retribution.

   (B) deterrence.

   (C) rehabilitation.

   (D) incapacitation.

At a federal sentencing hearing, the judge must afford the right of allocution.

173. What is allocution?

   (A) defense counsel may interrogate prosecution witnesses.

   (B) the jury has the opportunity to ask the court to clarify jury instructions.

   (C) the defendant has the right to address the court concerning the sentence.

   (D) the prosecutor, as a representative of the community, gets to express the community's position on the proper sentence.

174. As the result of the *Apprendi* line of cases, which of the following is CORRECT?

   (A) juries must find any facts that increase the statutory maximum or minimum sentences.

   (B) juries must find any facts that increase the statutory maximum but not the statutory minimum sentences.

   (C) juries must find any facts that increase the statutory minimum but not the statutory maximum sentences.

   (D) juries must impose sentence in all cases when the sentence involves taking into consideration any statutory factors.

You are a federal probation officer who was just assigned to prepare a presentence report on a person convicted of many serious drug offenses and is widely known to be ruthless with his enemies. You are concerned that the defendant will be vindictive toward some of the people who you hope will speak candidly with you about the defendant. You know that Rule 32, Federal Rules of Criminal

Procedure, requires you to provide the defense with a copy of the presentence report over a month before the sentencing hearing.

175. Under Rule 32, what may you do to protect these people providing negative information for your report?

ANSWER:

176. At a federal sentencing hearing, which of the following is NOT entitled to address the court?

(A) the convicted person.

(B) defense counsel.

(C) the crime victim.

(D) people from the community with a "strong legitimate interest" in the case.

177. At a federal sentencing hearing, which of the following rules are followed?

(A) the exclusionary rule so that evidence obtained in violation of the Fourth Amendment is not admissible.

(B) the Federal Rules of Evidence.

(C) the accused's right to confront sources of adverse information.

(D) none of above is required.

Three years ago, the newly-elected Governor of your state acted on her promise to "get rid of child porn now and forever." At the governor's insistence, the legislature passed a new law increasing the penalty for first-time possession of child porn from a minimum of five years to, under the new law, a maximum of 50 years.

You are an appellate court assigned a case of a 22-year-old man with no criminal record, a new wife and a steady job who was convicted of possession of a porn video involving a three-year-old girl and sentenced to a 25-year prison term under the new law. Defense counsel has appealed the sentence as violating the Eighth Amendment's Cruel and Unusual Punishment Clause.

178. What is your response to the argument?

ANSWER:

Bob "Pit Bull" Pitler was convicted in federal court of seven counts of conspiracy to traffic in drugs and 22 substantive drug offenses. He maintains that the convictions should be overturned because devastating evidence obtained in an illegal interrogation in violation of the Fifth and Sixth Amendments was introduced at his federal trial.

His defense counsel unsuccessfully challenged the evidence in the trial court, then failed in an appeal to the appropriate federal circuit court. The U.S. Supreme Court refused to consider the case. Defense counsel now wants to pursue collateral relief on the theory that Pitler's federal constitutional rights were violated when the federal court admitted evidence obtained in the interrogation.

179. Which of the following avenues for possible relief should ordinarily be used?

(A) federal habeas corpus.

(B) motion to vacate sentence under 28 U.S.C. § 2255.

(C) appeal to the state supreme court in the state where the conviction occurred.

(D) state habeas corpus.

After a lengthy trial, Khaleel Mostuma was convicted in State B of smuggling untaxed cigarettes into the state. Defense counsel unsuccessfully objected to jury instructions on the definition of reasonable doubt. Appeals to the State B intermediate and supreme courts also failed. The defense lawyer now will file a federal habeas corpus petition contesting the jury instructions.

180. Where should the federal habeas corpus petition be filed?

(A) in Washington, D.C., where the Supreme Court of the United States is located.

(B) in a State B trial court in the judicial district where the trial occurred.

(C) in a federal district court in the judicial district where the state supreme court is located.

(D) in a federal district court in the judicial district where Mostuma is incarcerated.

181. Which of the following would preclude a federal court from considering a petition for a writ of habeas corpus from a state prisoner?

(A) the same claim was presented in a prior federal habeas corpus application.

(B) the defendant has not yet completed service of the sentence imposed for the conviction allegedly obtained in violation of the United States Constitution.

(C) the state judgment became final six months ago when the period for direct appeal under state law expired.

(D) the state prisoner's petition alleges a violation of the United States Constitution rather than the constitution of the state where the conviction occurred.

You have been hired to represent Shlomo Blumberg who was convicted in a federal court of seven counts of identity theft for his involvement in a scheme to obtain and use stolen credit card information. At trial, another lawyer argued that Blumberg's Fifth Amendment rights were violated by police interrogation at his home. The trial court rejected the argument as did the circuit court and the Supreme Court declined to review the matter. The trial lawyer also lost a motion to vacate the conviction under 28 U.S.C. § 2255.

You want to file a second motion to vacate presenting a better researched argument that the trial court made a fatal error in using a jury selection procedure that eliminated elderly citizens from being included on the venire.

182. Which if any of the following must you establish in order to have a chance at having the second motion to vacate granted by the federal court?

(A) the claim was actually presented in the first motion to vacate, but the federal judge incorrectly rejected it as lacking merit.

(B) the claim was not presented in the first motion to vacate because counsel did not discover the jury selection error until after Blumberg was convicted.

(C) the case law that was violated by the jury selection system had been in place over 20 years and the district court should have been aware of it when selecting Blumberg's jury pool.

(D) none of above would be helpful.

183. Which of the following is INCORRECT about federal habeas corpus:

(A) a habeas corpus petitioner can file as many petitions as she wishes so long as she raises different issues in each petition.

(B) any judge on the court of appeals may issue a certificate of appeability authorizing an appeal on a claim in the habeas petition.

(C) ineffective assistance of state post-conviction counsel can constitute cause and prejudice to permit a habeas court to review the merits of an otherwise defaulted claim.

(D) none of above is incorrect.

You represent a state prisoner challenging a state conviction. Within one year of the Supreme Court of the United States denying the petition for writ of certiorari to review the state post-conviction judgment, you filed your federal habeas corpus petition alleging numerous federal constitutional violations during the state prisoner's trial. The state attorney general filed a motion to dismiss the petition asserting that the case was filed beyond the statute of limitations in 28 U.S.C. § 2244(d) because the petition was filed more than one year after the state supreme court denied review in state post-conviction.

184. The district court should:

    (A) dismiss the petition as untimely.

    (B) deny the motion to dismiss, find the petition to be filed timely, and proceed to the merits.

    (C) find the petition to be untimely but grant equitable tolling of the statute of limitations based on fundamental fairness.

    (D) find the petition to be untimely but deny the motion to dismiss because the petition contains arguably meritorious claims.

A new client, Carla Fuentes, was recently convicted of arson by a state court jury and was sentenced to five years in state prison. Trial counsel appealed unsuccessfully to the state intermediate appellate court. The state supreme court denied discretionary review. When Fuentes' lawyer died suddenly, you were retained to represent her. You are considering filing a federal habeas corpus petition to challenge the state conviction. You begin your study of the huge case file. You know that federal habeas corpus law requires that, in most cases, the petitioner must have "exhausted" available state remedies.

185. What must you look for in the file to assess whether this occurred?

ANSWER:

Assume that your review of the file showed that the issue you want to raise in a federal habeas corpus petition — the admissibility of a confession under *Miranda v. Arizona* — was already raised unsuccessfully by appellate counsel on direct appeal in state court. The state court determined that the *Miranda* warnings were valid and the confession was admissible.

186. How will this state appellate decision affect your federal habeas corpus petition?

ANSWER:

You are appointed to represent Bethany Doomer, an indigent person convicted of prostitution. After a thorough review of the trial record, you consult with Ms. Doomer about her appeal. You advise her that, despite your best efforts to find appellate issues, you can find no meritorious claims to raise. Ms. Doomer understands but asks that you file an appellate brief on her behalf.

187. Which of the following is the best course for you to follow as an ethical lawyer?

    (A) inform your client that you refuse to file anything in any court.

(B) file a brief in the appellate court raising issues that are colorable appellate issues, albeit issues that you believe are not meritorious.

(C) send a letter to the appellate and trial courts informing them that you have withdrawn from representing your client.

(D) file an appellate brief arguing issues that you believe are frivolous but which you present as serious issues, hoping that the appellate court will somehow agree with you.

PRACTICE FINAL EXAM: QUESTIONS

MULTIPLE CHOICE

Your client, Pedro Gonzalez, an illegal immigrant from Mexico, was arrested for a drug sale when an undercover police officer bought a baggie of marijuana from your client who was selling it on a street corner. While ordinarily marijuana sales are handled by a plea to a minor misdemeanor and the charges were eventually dropped after a few months of law-abiding behavior, in this case the prosecutor charged your client with a felony because, the prosecutor stated on the evening news, "we have to get these illegal Mexicans in prison so the streets are safe for real Americans."

188. Which of the following would be your best defense to the marijuana charge?

(A) entrapment.

(B) First Amendment.

(C) equal protection.

(D) double jeopardy since your client could be deported if convicted of the marijuana charge.

189. Assuming each of the following actually occurs in a case regulated by the Federal Rules of Criminal Procedure, which would likely occur THIRD?

(A) arraignment (Rule 10).

(B) complaint (Rule 3).

(C) indictment (Rule 7).

(D) preliminary hearing (Rule 5.1).

190. Under the Federal Rules, if a person is arrested and taken to jail without an arrest warrant having been issued, the lack of this warrant necessitates which of the following procedures?

(A) initial appearance.

(B) grand jury.

(C) preliminary hearing.

(D) *Gerstein* hearing.

Shelly Malone was arrested by state authorities for auto theft after a burglar, Sammy Knight, was arrested and, in exchange for a lenient sentence, told the police about Malone's car theft. Malone was accorded a bail hearing once counsel was appointed at the initial appearance. The day before the bail hearing, Malone told a cellmate that the "scumbag who ratted on me will never make it to testify at trial."

At the bail hearing, the cellmate repeated what Malone had said and the trial court denied release on bail pending trial, finding that Malone posed a danger to the safety of the main prosecution witness. State law permitted pretrial detention to protect the life of potential witnesses.

191. The state law authorizing pretrial detention to protect the safety of potential witnesses is:

    (A) constitutional under the Eighth Amendment's excessive bail provision.

    (B) unconstitutional under the Eighth Amendment's excessive bail provision.

    (C) unconstitutional under the Due Process Clause.

    (D) illegal under the Bail Reform Act of 1984.

192. In a jurisdiction based on the Federal Rules of Criminal Procedure, which is NOT true about the preliminary hearing?

    (A) the beyond a reasonable doubt standard is used.

    (B) the proceeding is adversarial, ordinarily with a prosecutor and defense lawyer representing the two sides.

    (C) the rules of evidence do not apply.

    (D) the accused may choose to testify.

Your client was sentenced to federal prison for three years after being convicted of money laundering in federal court. She now seeks release pending appeal.

193. Under the Bail Reform Act of 1984, what must you establish by clear and convincing evidence in order to have your client released pending appeal?

    (A) she is not likely to flee.

    (B) she is not likely to pose a danger to the safety of the community.

    (C) the appeal raises a substantial question of law or fact likely to result in reversal or a new trial.

    (D) all of above.

You are a legislator in a state that is streamlining its criminal procedures. Currently, a state statute gives the criminal accused the right to a grand jury hearing for all felonies. The state constitution is silent on the issue. Many legislators want to eliminate the grand jury because a recent study showed that it delayed trials by almost four months and costs several million dollars to fund statewide.

194. Can your state legislature constitutionally eliminate the grand jury?

(A) Yes, for all crimes except capital crimes where due process requires grand jury consideration.

(B) Yes, for all crimes.

(C) No, the Due Process Clause requires grand jury approval for all felonies.

(D) No, the Fifth Amendment requires grand jury approval for all crimes unless waived by the accused.

You represent a lawyer charged with knowingly filing a false tax return by failing to report $25,000 in income. Your client assures you that he did not know he was supposed to report the income which was from a bet he won while in Las Vegas for a convention. He took a lie detector test from a very reputable expert which showed he was telling the truth when he said he did not know he was to include the gambling gain on his tax forms. You gave the lie detector results to the prosecuting attorney and asked that the grand jury be given copies. The prosecutor refused to share the information with the grand jury because "we choose the proof for the grand jury; defense counsel does not."

You filed a Motion to Dismiss the Indictment for Failure to Provide Exculpatory Information to the Grand Jury.

195. Under the United States Constitution, your motion will be:

(A) granted since the defendant's due process rights were violated.

(B) denied since the accused has no right to have the grand jury consider exculpatory information.

(C) granted because under the Fifth Amendment's grand jury provision, the government must give reliable exculpatory information to the grand jury.

(D) denied because the defendant should have given the exculpatory proof to the judge rather than to the district attorney.

You are a law clerk for United States District Judge Wilbur who has asked you to review a federal indictment that is being challenged as being constitutionally infirm.

196. Which of the following is TRUE about an indictment in federal felony cases under Rule 7 of the Federal Rules of Criminal Procedure?

(A) the prosecutor in a felony case may proceed by either indictment or information without the defendant's consent.

(B) at any time the prosecutor may strike "surplusage" (*i.e.*, unnecessary language) from the wording of an indictment so the document is more easily understood by jurors.

(C) an indictment must contain the essential facts of the offense charged.

(D) the defendant's legal name must be included in the indictment.

Robert was charged in one indictment with (1) possession of a weapon by a convicted felon, (2) drug possession with intent to sell, and (3) extortion. The charges stemmed from Robert's sale of cocaine to an undercover agent. Robert threatened to shoot the agent if she testified against him. The gun — a pistol — was found during a lawful search of Robert's home.

197. Under Federal Rule of Criminal Procedure 8(a), is joinder of these three crimes permissible in one trial?

(A) joinder is permissible because they were of the same or similar character.

(B) joinder is permissible because they were based on the same act or transaction.

(C) joinder is permissible because they were part of a common scheme or plan.

(D) joinder is impermissible.

The state prosecutors' association has drafted a bill to change discovery rules that have long required the government to turn over certain materials to the defense. The new rules provide that neither the prosecution nor defense has to provide the other with any discovery at all. Each side is left to its own devices to obtain information needed to prepare for the case.

198. The new rule is:

(A) constitutional since it treats both sides the same.

(B) constitutional because the legislature is free to establish the rules of criminal procedure, including discovery.

(C) unconstitutional because due process requires significant reciprocal discovery to provide a fair trial for both sides.

(D) unconstitutional because the prosecution must turn over information to the defense that would be helpful to either guilt or sentence.

On January 1, 2009, Kathleen Browning received stolen property from a neighbor who was a burglar. Browning was arrested on January 1, 2010, indicted for receiving stolen property on July 2, 2010, and convicted in a one-day trial on January 5, 2011. She seeks to overturn the conviction.

199. Which of the following theories would MOST LIKELY be viable in reversing the conviction?

(A) due process because of the one-year delay between the crime and the arrest.

(B) constitutional speedy trial because of the six-month delay between arrest and indictment.

(C) statute of limitations because of the six-month delay between indictment and trial.

(D) none of above would be a viable theory to overturn the conviction.

Melanie, a resident of Silver County, is on vacation at a lake in Scott County. She gets in an argument with Francie, another vacationer who is intoxicated and lives in Knox County. Francie pushes Melanie who falls down and breaks her arm.

200. In the usual case, which of the following is the proper venue for the trial of Francie for assault, assuming the defendant has not moved for a venue change?

    (A) Silver County where the victim lives.

    (B) Knox County where the defendant lives.

    (C) Scott County where the alleged assault occurred.

    (D) All of above are appropriate.

You represent a man charged with the torture-killing of a three-year-old child abducted from a child care facility. The national press has turned the case into a media circus with reporters from all over the world publishing daily updates. You fear that this attention will make it impossible to have the jury be unbiased during the trial. To minimize this risk, you have filed a Motion to Exclude the Press and Public from the trial. Your motion includes a signed affidavit from the defendant waiving his right to a public trial. The government opposes your closure motion.

201. Based on the facts above, the motion will be:

    (A) granted because the defendant has a due process right to a fair trial and this right is superior to other rights.

    (B) granted because the Sixth Amendment right to a public trial is for the defendant's benefit and the defendant may waive it, which occurred here.

    (C) denied because the press and public have a First and Fourteenth Amendment right to attend a criminal trial.

    (D) denied because the government is entitled to a public trial and the court may not close a courtroom if the government wants a public trial.

In order to save money, a state legislature is considering reducing the number of jurors in a misdemeanor trial to 10 but maintaining the requirement that guilt be found unanimously. The state constitution mandates a jury of 12 in felony cases but is silent about misdemeanor cases.

202. The new statute reducing the number of jurors from 12 to 10 in misdemeanor cases is

    (A) constitutional since under the separation of powers doctrine states are free to set the number of jurors in all cases.

    (B) constitutional under the Sixth Amendment to the U.S. Constitution.

    (C) unconstitutional under the Sixth Amendment to the U.S. Constitution.

    (D) unconstitutional under due process ensured by the U.S. Constitution.

Judge Kathleen Nobuku is presiding over a difficult five-month state criminal fraud case. Both sides have offered substantial proof. State law requires a unanimous verdict for a conviction or acquittal. After three days of jury deliberation, the jury foreperson gave Judge Nobuku a note saying, "We are deadlocked on the case. I do not know if we can ever reach a verdict one way or the other." Judge Nobuku has decided she wants the jurors to continue deliberating but wants to put a bit of pressure on them to reach a verdict. State law gives her much flexibility in the decision.

203. What should Judge Nobuku do?

(A) give the jurors an *Allen* charge urging them to continue deliberations and to listen carefully to the views of other jurors.

(B) find out the split of tentative juror votes and award the verdict to the side that had an overwhelming majority of the votes.

(C) declare a mistrial so the case can be retried and reach a verdict.

(D) replace all the jurors with alternates and instruct the new jurors to start from scratch in deliberating on the case.

You are defense counsel to a woman charged with embezzlement from her employer. Trial is scheduled to start tomorrow morning. Jury selection has been going on for two days. Five jurors have been selected. A few minutes ago you received a call from the court clerk telling you that the trial will be cancelled because a virus has been detected among the five selected jurors and the judge fears the entire jury could be infected if the trial went ahead. You were told the judge has dismissed the five accepted jurors and will hold a hearing in a week to set a new trial date.

You have filed a Motion to Dismiss Charges Because of Double Jeopardy.

204. How should the court rule on the motion?

(A) grant the motion because jury selection had begun and the state gets only one chance to convict a citizen, according to the Double Jeopardy Clause.

(B) grant the motion because the defendant was not even consulted and did not consent to the trial cancellation.

(C) deny the motion because the full jury had not been selected.

(D) deny the motion because the Double Jeopardy Clause is inapplicable.

205. Which of the following will NOT routinely result in a potential juror in a child molestation case being excluded for cause from serving on the jury:

(A) exposure to pretrial publicity.

(B) awaiting trial on a serious misdemeanor in the same jurisdiction.

(C) being the defendant's common law husband.

(D) being the victim's Sunday school teacher.

You are an experienced civil litigator who has been appointed to represent an arsonist in a criminal case. Your client denies setting the fire. You are quite familiar with discovery in civil cases and want to depose three possible witnesses to the arson. You think they may have seen the arsonist and could possibly be good defense witnesses.

206. Under the Federal Rules of Criminal Procedure, your efforts to depose the three witnesses under Rule 15 are likely to be:

(A) unsuccessful since depositions are not permitted in criminal cases.

(B) unsuccessful because you cannot use the deposition in criminal cases for discovery.

(C) successful because one or more of these witnesses may turn out to be critical defenses witnesses.

(D) successful only if the prosecution agrees to the depositions.

207. If a hearsay statement in a recorded statement to police is found to be "testimonial" and therefore covered by the Confrontation Clause of the Sixth Amendment, which of the following is NOT necessary in order for the statement to be admissible against the criminal accused at trial?

(A) the declarant who made the statement must be unavailable.

(B) the declarant must have been subject to cross examination about the testimonial statement.

(C) the statement must be hearsay.

(D) the defendant must have been present when the statement was made.

208. Which of the following is/are unlimited in number?

(A) challenges for cause.

(B) peremptory challenges.

(C) all of above.

(D) none of above.

Beatrice Holzman was arrested after postal authorities discovered a mail bomb had been sent to Judge Ramos, who had presided over Holzman's trial four years ago for auto theft. Holzman had threatened to "get even" many times. Holzman is charged with the following federal crime:

> Section A-46. Sending a Destructive Device. Whoever, with intent to cause physical injury, sends a destructive device through the mail shall be guilty of a felony punishable by a maximum of 10 years in prison.

Last year, Holzman was convicted in federal court of attempted first degree murder for exactly the same incident involving mailing the bomb to Judge Ramos. The prosecution brought the new case because it believed Holzman's sentence for the attempted murder conviction was too lenient.

Defense counsel in the current destructive device case has filed a Motion to Dismiss Because of Double Jeopardy, arguing that the conviction last year for attempted murder bars prosecution for the destructive device charge.

209. You are the federal judge handling the current case. How will you rule on the motion?

ANSWER:

You represent LaVon Williams, a difficult client who attended two years of law school and thinks he is very familiar with the law. Williams hired you after firing his original lawyer who represented Williams in proceedings leading up to a guilty plea.

Four months ago, Williams was high on drugs and became violent when asked to leave a bar at 2:00 a.m. He attacked the bouncer with a beer bottle, was arrested and charged with aggravated assault. The entire altercation was captured by the security camera.

The maximum possible sentence in the jurisdiction is 10 years in prison. The prosecution agreed to allow Williams to plead guilty to "ordinary" assault and be sentenced to six months in jail. At the hearing where your client entered a plea, the following colloquy occurred:

Judge: Mr. Williams, are you ready to enter a plea?

Defendant: Yes, your honor.

Judge: I won't waste your time here, today. Have you discussed this with your lawyer?

Defendant: Yes, your honor. He's an idiot.

Judge: And do you want to plead? I understand the prosecution has offered you six months in jail if you plead guilty to assault.

Defendant: Yes, that's about it.

Judge: Do you know that if you plead, you waive many issues, such as the right to have a trial and the right to remain silent?

Defendant: Of course I do. I went to law school.

Judge: OK. Did you study criminal procedure?

Defendant: Of course, I am not uninformed.

Judge: OK. Counsel, have you discussed the various rights with your client?

Defendant: Ask me, not that fool. We didn't discuss nothing. He's an idiot and so are you.

Judge: Mr. Williams, I accept your plea and sentence you to six months in jail consistent with the deal you worked out with the government.

Williams has now had two weeks to think about the deal and has decided it was a lousy one because he actually used the beer bottle in self-defense when the bouncer attacked him. He wants to withdraw his plea and has hired you to represent him.

210. How do you assess the validity of his plea and the likelihood of having the plea withdrawn?

ANSWER:

You are selecting the jury in your client Melvin's trial for second degree reckless murder allegedly caused by your client's sale of tainted moonshine to the victim. You think that people who have imbibed moonshine would be excellent jurors since they appreciate that buyers of moonshine accept the risk that the substance will be poisonous because they know that the government will not permit it to be made openly and in a totally safe environment. You begin exercising your peremptory challenges to exclude anyone who has not consumed moonshine. The prosecution makes a *Batson* objection on the theory that you are excluding the most educated jurors.

211. What ruling should the court make?

ANSWER:

Bartlett Fryer was convicted of first degree murder in a murder that occurred in a remote corner of a shopping center parking lot. A person exiting the lot saw a man throw the victim to the ground and attack her. At trial this witness clearly identified Fryer as the man whom she saw. Fryer denies involvement with the incident.

You are defense counsel. The victim had some dirt and other matter under her fingernails but police were unable to get any usable information from their analysis of it. You have been researching the possible use of DNA analysis to exonerate your client using a newly refined method of assessing human DNA. You filed a motion to permit the fingernail material to be analyzed by an independent lab that had discovered the new approach. Today, you received a letter indicating that the police had "lost" the fingernail scrapings and were unlikely to find the evidence. The letter indicated it may have been inadvertently thrown in the trash by a custodian, though no one knows for sure.

212. You file a Motion to Dismiss for Loss of Critical Evidence in Violation of Due Process. Assess the likely result of your motion.

ANSWER:

Sharon Davis is charged with intentional homicide for shooting Carl Icon, a local radio personality. Davis and Icon had long been lovers but broke up a month ago when Icon told Davis he had a new girlfriend.

Davis maintains that she did not kill Icon and does not know who did. A police search of Davis' apartment found a .22 caliber pistol that had been recently fired. During trial preparation, Davis' defense lawyer had forensic tests conducted on the .22 caliber bullet that killed Icon. The tests concluded that the bullet was fired from a .22 caliber pistol that did not come from Davis' weapon.

Davis' defense lawyer wants to know whether government lab tests concluded the same thing, but does not want to give the government the results of the defense-ordered tests, preferring to surprise the government with them at trial. Your jurisdiction has adopted the Federal Rules of Criminal Procedure.

213. You are a law clerk for defense counsel. Advise your boss.

ANSWER:

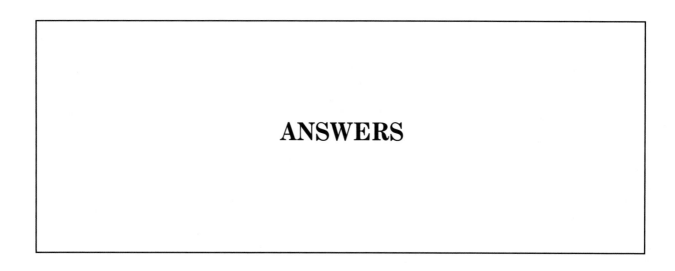

ANSWERS

1. **Answer (D) is correct.** The preliminary examination is held ordinarily 14–21 days after the initial appearance, according to Rule 5.1(c), making it the third event in the sequence. The grand jury is held after the preliminary examination. The first event could be an arrest; the second, an initial appearance. Rule 5.

   Answer (C) is incorrect. Though the order of proceedings in federal criminal cases does not necessarily follow a consistent pattern (for example, the defendant may be indicted, *then* arrested, etc.), if all procedures are followed the grand jury routinely considers a case *after* the preliminary examination, arrest, and initial appearance.

   Answer (A) is incorrect because an arrest would occur first. Then the initial appearance would be held.

   Answer (B) is incorrect. The initial appearance ordinarily occurs shortly after an arrest according to Federal Rule of Criminal Procedure 5, but before the preliminary examination and the grand jury.

2.   **Answer (D) is correct.** There are several doctrines that come into play that make Answer (D) the correct answer. Courts are extremely reluctant to interfere with prosecutorial discretion. The separation of powers doctrine is cited frequently as the basis for this "hands-off" approach. In *Inmates of Attica v. Rockefeller*, 477 F.2d 375 (2d Cir. 1973), the leading case, the Second Circuit held that courts would not order prosecutions, even if a state investigation of inmate grievances showed strong evidence of criminal wrongdoing and even if a statute "required" prosecution.

    Answer (A) is not the best answer. The *Attica* court and many others refuse to require the prosecution to make these discretionary decisions, even in good faith.

    Answer (B) is also not the best answer. Courts virtually never interfere with the grand jury's discretion or the prosecutor's decisions involving the grand jury. In some jurisdictions, a grand jury may return an indictment without the prosecutor's approval, and in a few states the state attorney general or governor may appoint a special prosecutor, but even in these jurisdictions the prosecutor may subsequently end the case by refusing to bring it to trial.

    Answer (C) is incorrect. Some states have a mechanism to transfer responsibility of certain cases from local prosecutors to specially appointed prosecutors. Prosecution decisions, however, are ordinarily an executive branch function, one that the courts rarely interfere with and that is beyond the scope of this question absent more information about state laws for appointment of special prosecutors. Therefore, **Answer (D) is the best answer.**

The only situation where the courts may intervene in a prosecutor's decision not to prosecute is where there is some indication that the prosecutor was involved in selective prosecution on the basis of an unconstitutional criterion, such as race, religion, or other arbitrary classification. *See U.S. v. Armstrong*, 517 U.S. 456 (1996). To obtain discovery to establish this claim, *Armstrong* would require the defense first to make a "credible showing of different treatment of similarly situated persons." In the hypothetical above, there is no evidence that the prosecutor used an unconstitutional criterion though she may well have been influenced by her personal knowledge of the alleged criminal.

3. This question concerns the elements of a valid complaint under Rule 3 of the Federal Rules of Criminal Procedure. The elements are: made under oath before a federal magistrate judge or, if a federal magistrate judge is unavailable, state judge. Case law adds an additional requirement: that the statement be signed by a U.S. Attorney.

Answer (C) is correct. Rule 3 requires a written statement made under oath of the essential facts and the charged offense(s), signed by a U.S. Attorney (case law). All these elements are satisfied in the scenario.

Answer (A) is incorrect. Rule 3 requires that the written statement must contain the "essential facts constituting the offense charged." This general statement lacks sufficient specificity to satisfy the "essential facts" standard. It also must have been signed by a U.S. Attorney, according to case law.

Answer (B) is incorrect. Rule 3 requires that the written statement be made under oath. No one swore to the validity of the information in the statement.

Answer (D) is incorrect. Rule 3 requires that the written statement of essential facts be made under oath, which did not occur in this case. It can be issued by a state or local judicial officer. It is also doubtful that a secretary in the U.S. Attorney's office could sign a court document on behalf of the U.S. Attorney.

4.   Rule 5(a)(1)(A) of the Federal Rules of Criminal Procedure states clearly that an officer arresting a person must take that person "without unnecessary delay" before a federal magistrate judge or, in some cases, to a state or local judicial officer for an initial appearance. This means that you must locate a judge and have Sophie brought before that person without too great a delay. The vague "without unnecessary delay" test of Rule 5(a) does allow some flexibility in the time of this process.

In addition to the timeliness of the initial appearance, you must also comply with the location requirement in Rule 5. Since Sophie was arrested in the same federal district where the crime occurred, under Rule 5(c)(1), Sophie should be brought to a judge in that district for the initial appearance.

5.   Under the new facts, the crime occurred in the Eastern District of State A but Sophie was arrested in the Western District of State A. Under Rule 5(c)(2), the initial appearance may be in the district of arrest (Western District) or in an adjacent district if the initial appearance could occur more promptly there or if the offense was allegedly committed there.

6.   If the arrest were made without a warrant, several procedures would be triggered. First, a complaint (Rule 4(a)) establishing probable cause must be filed promptly in the district where the crime was allegedly committed. Rule 5(b).

In addition, *Gerstein v. Pugh*, 420 U.S. 103 (1975), requires that the defendant arrested without a warrant be given a judicial hearing to assess probable cause for detention. This may be — and often is — combined with the initial appearance. *Gerstein* and later cases also mandate that the *Gerstein* probable cause hearing be held in a timely fashion. *County of Riverside v. McLaughlin*, 500 U.S. 44 (1991), says ordinarily the *Gerstein* hearing should be held within 48 hours of arrest. After that time, the government bears the burden of showing why the excessive delay occurred.

7.   **Answer D is correct as the best answer.** Rule 5(d), which prescribes procedures in federal initial appearances, mandates that defendant be given all of the listed rights.

Answers (A), (B), and (C), are incorrect though each is guaranteed individually by Rule 5(d).

8. **Answer (A) is correct.** The Eighth Amendment states, "Excessive bail shall not be required . . . ."

    Answer (B) is incorrect. It is well-accepted that the Eighth Amendment does not create any right to release on bail and certainly does not bar the denial of bail.

    Answer (C) is incorrect because the Eighth Amendment does not address indigent defendants.

    Answer (D) is incorrect. The Eighth Amendment also does not deal with the administration of the bail system. Thus, it does not deal at all with the use of professional bail bonding companies or with their power to apprehend people who abscond while on bail.

9. **Answer (B) is correct.** If Marvin uses a bail bonding company, he will have to pay its fee, which is usually about 10% of the total bond (*i.e.*, $500 on a $5,000 bond). Sometimes the bonding company also is permitted to charge various administrative fees as well. If Marvin shows up for all court appearances, he is not entitled to a refund from the bonding company. The 10% fee is kept by the company.

    Answer (A) is incorrect because if Marvin posts a cash bond of $5,000 when he appears as required, he will ordinarily get back all or most of the entire sum he deposited with the court.

    Answer (C) is incorrect because the property bond means that Marvin's real property will be released from any lien after he appears for court proceedings. The property bond means simply that if he does not appear, the property he uses for the bond could, in theory, be sold to satisfy his obligations for the bond. If he does appear, his property interests remain intact.

    Answer (D) is incorrect because an unsecured bond is simply a promise to pay a certain amount (here $5,000) if Marvin does not appear at the required proceedings. When Marvin does appear, he will not pay any sums.

10. A bail or bond schedule is a chart that sets a bail amount for particular crimes. For example, the schedule may provide a bail amount of $500 for shoplifting. Often, the schedule is located at the jail. A person arrested and brought to jail may get immediate release by satisfying the bail amount set in the schedule. Perhaps the alleged shoplifter would post the $500 in cash or, more likely, use a bail bond company which would guarantee the $500 amount and would be paid, usually, 10% of this amount as its fee. Some court systems also have adopted a bond schedule.

    The advantages are that it enables an arrestee such as Wylie to be released promptly and it treats virtually all people charged with the same crime the same way. The disadvantage is that the amount of bond it sets is not individualized to accommodate any arrestee's particular situation.

11.   **Answer (D) is correct** because Answers (A), (B), and (C) are all specifically mentioned in the Act as issues the court is to consider in its decision.

12.   **Answer (B) is correct.** Under 18 U.S.C. § 3142, in the usual case, the first choice is release on personal recognizance (or unsecured appearance bond).

      Answer (A) is incorrect because release on conditions is to be used only if release on personal recognizance will not assure the appearance of the person or the safety of the community. 18 U.S.C. § 3142(c). Immediate payment of restitution is not appropriate since guilt has not been established.

      Answer (C) is similarly incorrect because release on a secured bond is a release condition that is disfavored by the priority rule in Answer (B) above.

      Answer (D) is incorrect because temporary detention is authorized for someone on release from another offense, on probation or parole, or in the country illegally. 18 U.S.C. § 3142(d). Monique fits in none of the categories for which temporary detention is authorized.

13.   **Answer (C) is correct** because the Bail Reform Act of 1984, 18 U.S.C. § 3142(f), requires a judge who finds that no conditions will assure the safety of a person or the community, do so only when shown clear and convincing evidence of this fact.

      Answers (A), (B), and (D) are incorrect because the standard for conditions ensuring safety is clear and convincing evidence rather than probable cause (Answer (A), preponderance of the evidence (B), or beyond a reasonable doubt (D)).

14.   You should reject defense counsel's argument. In *U.S. v. Salerno*, 481 U.S. 739 (1987), the United States Supreme Court upheld the Bail Reform Act's provision authorizing pretrial detention if no release conditions will reasonably assure the safety of any other person and the community. The Court rejected the argument that detention was only permissible for fear of flight. The *Salerno* opinion stressed that detention was regulatory, not punitive. The opinion also noted that the government's interest in preventing crime by arrestees is legitimate and compelling and may be weightier than an individual's interests in pretrial freedom. Therefore, according to *Salerno*, the Due Process Clause does not bar the pretrial detention.

      Salerno also held that pretrial detention does not violate the Eighth Amendment's excessive bail provision since the detention is not excessive when balanced against the evil of individual or community harm.

15.   **Answer (C) is correct.** The Bail Reform Act does authorize release pending appeal if, among other findings, the appeal raises a substantial question of law or fact likely to result in a reversal or new trial.

      Answer (A) is incorrect. Release pending an appeal is authorized in limited circumstances.

      Answer (B) is incorrect because it states an incorrect standard for release pending appeal. The defense does not have to establish these facts beyond a reasonable doubt. Rather, the court must find them by clear and convincing evidence.

      Answer (D) is incorrect. The Eighth Amendment does not require setting a bail amount for a person convicted of a crime and awaiting appeal.

16. **Answer (A) is correct.** The Bail Reform Act does not permit detention when the witness's testimony could be procured by deposition.

Answers (B) and (C) are incorrect. Promises by either the witness or the witness's counsel that the witness will appear do not negate the Bail Reform Act's authorization for detention of witnesses.

Answer (D) is incorrect. The service of a subpoena does not negate the authority to hold the witness until a deposition or trial.

17. **Answer (D) is correct.** Under Rule 5.1, the felony defendant is entitled to a preliminary hearing unless it is waived or an indictment has been issued.

    Answer (A) is incorrect because an indictment does not trigger the need for a preliminary hearing. It actually eliminates the need for one in the federal system.

    Answer (B) is incorrect. The filing of an information does not dispense with the need for a preliminary hearing unless the defendant has consented to the information.

    Answer (C) is incorrect. The possibility of incarceration does not determine whether a preliminary hearing is mandated under Rule 5.1.

18. **Answer (B) is correct.** Rule 5.1(a) specifically provides that a preliminary hearing need not be conducted if an indictment has been issued.

    Answer (A) is incorrect. The defendant is given a right to a preliminary hearing in some circumstances. The prosecutor may not waive this proceeding, but may render it unnecessary by taking the case directly to the grand jury and obtaining an indictment.

    Answer (C) is incorrect. The preliminary hearing has nothing to do with whether or not the accused requests a jury trial. Indeed, this hearing is held long before such a request would be made.

    Answer (D) is incorrect. The defendant is entitled to a preliminary hearing under Rule 5.1 unless one of the exceptions applies. If the defendant misuses the hearing for discovery, the remedy is for the trial court to use its authority over the case to restrict defense counsel's inappropriate efforts. The court's contempt power may even be used when appropriate and necessary.

19. **Answer (C) is correct** (*i.e.*, it is untrue). No jury participates in a preliminary hearing; the judge alone conducts the hearing and decides all questions of fact and law.

    Answers (A), (B), and (D) are incorrect (*i.e.*, they are all true). A federal preliminary hearing is an adversary hearing (Answer (A)), during which the accused has the right to testify (Answer (B)), and to cross-examine prosecution witnesses (Rule 5.1(e) (Answer (D))).

20. **Answer (A) is correct.** Rule 5.1(e) states that the defendant "may introduce evidence but may not object to evidence on the ground that it was unlawfully acquired." Therefore, the defendant cannot challenge the constitutional legality of the acquisition of evidence during the federal preliminary hearing.

    Answer (B) is incorrect. The evidentiary rules apply in trial situations, and are relaxed for the preliminary hearing proceedings.

    Answer (C) is incorrect. Rule 5.1(f) states: "[i]f the magistrate judge finds no probable cause to believe an offense has been committed or the defendant committed it, the magistrate judge must dismiss the complaint and discharge the defendant." As such, the judge must discharge the defendant when there is no probable cause. Rule 5.1(f) also provides the government may still prosecute the defendant for the same offense, despite the finding of no probable cause.

Answer (D) is incorrect. Rule 5.1(c) states: "[t]he magistrate judge must hold the preliminary hearing within a reasonable time, but no later than 14 days after the initial appearance if the defendant is in custody and no later than 21 days if not in custody." As such, a 30-day delay violates this provision.

21.   **Answer (A) is correct.** Under Rule 5.1(e) of the Federal Rules of Criminal Procedure, the standard of proof in a preliminary hearing is whether the evidence made it appear to the judge that there is probable cause to believe that an offense was committed by the defendant.

Answer (B) is incorrect because the beyond-a-reasonable-doubt standard is for the criminal trial, not the preliminary hearing.

Answer (C) is incorrect because the defense does not have to prove the defendant's innocence; the prosecution must satisfy the probable cause standard.

Answer (D) is incorrect because the prosecution need not use its best witnesses at a preliminary hearing; it need only satisfy the probable cause standard. The judge is to consider the witnesses actually presented at the preliminary hearing, not those that the prosecution could have produced had it chosen to do so.

22.   Unfortunately for the defense, under Rule 5.1(e) of the Federal Rules of Criminal Procedure and Rule 1101(d)(3) of the Federal Rules of Evidence, the admissibility of evidence in a preliminary hearing differs markedly from that in a criminal trial. The intercepted cell phone conversations are likely admissible despite being obtained in violation of the Constitution and offered in violation of the rules of evidence.

In the federal system, evidence seized in violation of the Constitution may be admitted at a preliminary hearing since the exclusionary rule does not apply to that proceeding, according to Rule 5.1(e). In addition, Rule 1101(d)(3) of the Federal Rules of Evidence provides that the rules of evidence do not apply to a preliminary hearing. This means that hearsay evidence, though inadmissible in a criminal trial, may be admitted at a preliminary hearing. Some states take a different approach, applying their constitutional exclusionary rules and ordinary evidence rules to preliminary hearings.

23.   **Answer (D) is the best answer.** I, III, and IV are all appropriate actions in most jurisdictions that use a grand jury and have no statutes dealing with the four possible options.

    Answers (A) and (C) are therefore incorrect. The grand jury procedure is controlled by the prosecutor who, in many jurisdictions, may resubmit a case to the same grand jury or a different grand jury. Like other constitutional rights, the right to a grand jury can be waived by the defendant. Thus, Mr. Pierson, through counsel, may waive the grand jury and agree to have the case prosecuted by information. In such an instance, the prosecutor would file an information which has the same legal status as an indictment or presentment returned by a grand jury.

    Answer (B) is incorrect because jeopardy does not attach at the grand jury stage.

24.   **Answer (B) is correct.** Under Federal Rule of Criminal Procedure 6(f), a grand jury may indict only with the concurrence of at least 12 jurors. Therefore, **Answers (A), (C), and (D) are incorrect.**

25.   **Answer (B) is the only correct answer.** Under Federal Criminal Rule 6(a)(1), a federal grand jury must have 16–23 members. Therefore, **Answers (A), (C), and (D) are incorrect.**

26.   The challenge will likely be unsuccessful. Although grand jury proceedings are, in general, considered to be conducted in secret, Federal Rule of Criminal Procedure Rule 6(d)(1) recognizes that some people other than grand jurors may be present to facilitate the orderly work of the grand jury. These include the federal prosecutor, a language interpreter when needed to assist the witness, and a court reporter.

27.   **Answer (C) is correct.** The defendant's request for a jury trial does not bar a preliminary hearing. Under Federal Rule 5.1(a), a federal defendant charged with an offense other than a petty offense is entitled to a preliminary hearing before a magistrate judge unless the defendant waives the hearing, the defendant is indicted, the government files an information charging the defendant with a felony or misdemeanor, or the defendant is charged with a misdemeanor and consents to a trial before a magistrate judge.

    Answer (A) is incorrect because an indictment precludes a preliminary hearing.

    Answer (B) is incorrect because a defendant is not entitled to a preliminary hearing if he or she is charged with a misdemeanor and consents to be tried by a magistrate judge.

    Answer (D) is incorrect since a valid information replaces a preliminary hearing.

28.   **Answer (A) is correct.** Rule 6(e)(2) of the Federal Rules of Criminal Procedure imposes a general obligation of secrecy on a list of people involved with a federal grand jury. Grand jury witnesses are not included in this list and are not subject to any duty of secrecy.

Answers (B), (C), and (D) are incorrect because each of these categories of grand jury participants is specifically subjected to a general obligation of secrecy under Rule 6(e)(2).

29.   **Answer (D) is correct.** Under Federal Rule of Criminal Procedure 6(e), grand jury secrecy is not absolute. Disclosure is permitted to a number of people. **Answer (D) is the best answer** because the Rule does not authorize the indicted person to penetrate grand jury secrecy, although Rule 6(e)(3)(E)(ii) does permit the court to order disclosure to defense counsel upon a showing that grounds may exist for a motion to dismiss the indictment because of matters occurring before the grand jury.

Answers (A), (B), and (C) are incorrect. Rule 6(e) specifically permits disclosure to an attorney for the government for use in performing her duties (Answer (A)), an investigator assisting that government lawyer (Answer (B)), and a state government official who is assisting a federal attorney in investigating a violation of federal law (Answer (C)).

30.   **Answer (C) is correct** (*i.e.*, it is untrue). It is the only answer that is untrue; all other responses are true. Rule 6(e) mandates that all grand jury proceedings must be recorded by a court reporter or other suitable recording device. This includes testimony by witnesses, which is to be recorded.

Answer (A) is incorrect (*i.e.*, it is true) because the Federal Rules of Evidence do not apply to grand jury proceedings. *See Costello v. U.S.*, 350 U.S. 359 (1956); Federal Rule of Evidence 1101(d)(2) (Federal Rules of Evidence, other than privileges, do not apply in grand jury proceedings). Evidence inadmissible under the Federal Rules of Evidence may be heard and considered by grand jurors.

Answer (B) is incorrect (*i.e.*, it is true) because Rule 6(e)(4) of the Federal Rules of Criminal Procedure specifically authorizes a sealed indictment.

Answer (D) is incorrect (*i.e.*, it is true). Grand jury proceedings must not be recorded when the grand jury is deliberating or voting. Rule 6(e)(1).

31. **Answer (C) is correct.** Under Rule 7(f) of the Federal Rules of Criminal Procedure and similar rules in many jurisdictions, a Bill of Particulars is sought by defense counsel from the government in order to obtain more information about a vague indictment.

    Answer (A) is incorrect because this "bill" has nothing to do with money or a quantitative measure of professional services.

    Answer (B) is incorrect because the Bill of Particulars is a request by the defense, not the prosecution.

    Answer (D) is incorrect because a Bill of Particulars is only designed to assist the defense in preparing for trial, not for assisting the judge in his or her scheduling.

32. **Answer (D) is correct.** A Bill of Particulars is within the trial court's discretion. Rule 7(f) ("The court *may* direct the government to file a bill of particulars").

    Answer (A) is incorrect because the government, not the defense, files a Bill of Particulars.

    Answer (B) is incorrect because Rule 7(f) specifically says that a Bill of Particulars may be amended when justice requires.

    Answer (C) is incorrect because a Bill of Particulars does not make an invalid indictment valid. This is because the indictment is issued by a grand jury and the grand jury must make the decisions about its significant contents. A prosecutor, who prepares the Bill of Particulars, cannot amend an indictment.

33. A defendant who wants more detailed information than provided in the indictment may file a timely motion for a Bill of Particulars. Pursuant to Rule 7(f) of the Federal Rules of Criminal Procedure, the defendant may move for a Bill of Particulars before arraignment, within 14 days of arraignment or any time later that the court permits.

    The primary function of the Bill of Particulars is to inform the defendant of the nature of the crimes against him or her. Specifically, it informs the defendant about the essential facts of the crimes for which the defendant has been indicted. The situation described in the question is a good illustration since the charges are so general that the defense does not know which specific acts are alleged to have violated federal criminal laws.

    Additional helpful functions of the Bill of Particulars include enabling the defendant to prepare a defense, avoid double jeopardy, and lessen surprise for the defendant at trial.

34. **Answer (D) is correct.** A federal misdemeanor may be initiated by indictment, information, or complaint. Rule 58(b).

    Answers (A), (B), and (C) all represent valid ways for proceeding with a misdemeanor prosecution but answer (D) is best because all three methods are permissible.

35. **Answer (C) is correct.** A federal indictment need not be signed by defense counsel.

Answers (A), (B), and (D) are incorrect. Under Federal Rule of Criminal Procedure 7(c)(1), an indictment must be in writing (Answer (A)), cite the statute allegedly violated (Answer (B)), and be signed by an attorney for the government (Answer (D)).

36. You will probably be unsuccessful. In *U.S. v. Williams*, 504 U.S. 36 (1992), the United States Supreme Court held that a prosecutor had no duty to provide the grand jury with exculpatory statements about the alleged crime. The Court noted that the grand jury's responsibility is not to determine guilt or innocence, but rather to assess whether the evidence provides an adequate basis to bring criminal charges. Neither the grand jury guarantee of the Fifth Amendment nor the Supreme Court's supervisory power mandates that prosecutors must disclose exculpatory evidence to the grand jury. The law in a few states, however, does obligate the prosecutor to share exculpatory information with grand jurors.

37. **Answer (C) is clearly correct.** An indictment is not mandatory for prosecution of a crime punishable by a prison sentence of one year or less, making Answer (C) the correct choice. Federal Rule of Criminal Procedure 7(a)(1)(B). Federal Rule 58 provides that misdemeanors may be prosecuted by complaint, indictment, or information.

Answers (A) and (B) are incorrect. Under Federal Rule of Criminal Procedure 7(a), an indictment, unless waived, is required for the prosecution of a crime *punishable* by death or imprisonment for more than one year. Note that the key is the authorized punishment, not the actual punishment.

Answer (D) is not the best answer. Though it is true that virtually all federal felonies must be initiated by an indictment (unless waived), the yardstick is the maximum *punishment*, not whether the crime is a felony or misdemeanor. If the punishment — irrespective of the category of the crime — is more than one year in prison (as are felonies in virtually every jurisdiction), an indictment is needed under the Federal Rules of Criminal Procedure.

38. The success of your challenge will depend on state rather than federal law. The United States Supreme Court in *Hurtado v. California*, 110 U.S. 516 (1884) held that the Fifth Amendment's grand jury guarantee does not apply to the states. Therefore, states do not have to utilize a grand jury and a large number have rejected this procedure.

As a matter of state constitutional or statutory law, however, a number of states have retained the right to a grand jury, at least in felony cases. The challenge to the use of an information rather than an indictment for your client will hinge on whether state law mandated an indictment in this particular type of case. The facts in the question suggest that your state has not adopted the grand jury as part of its criminal justice process.

39. **Answer (C) is correct.** Under Rule 47 of the Federal Rules of Criminal Procedure, a party may support a pretrial motion by affidavit but does not have to do so; it is optional.

Answers (A), (B), and (D) are all incorrect because each is required by Rule 47.

40. Rule 12, Federal Rules of Criminal Procedure, provides a list of motions that must be filed pretrial.

Answer (A) is correct because Rule 12 does not establish a time limit for a Motion to Admit Evidence. Note that a Motion to Suppress Evidence ordinarily must be filed pretrial.

Answers (B) and (C) are incorrect because Federal Rule of Criminal Procedure 12(b) specifically says that a Motion to Suppress Evidence (Answer (B)) and a Motion to Sever Charges (Answer (C)) must be raised prior to trial.

Answer (D) is incorrect because a Motion to Dismiss Indictment for Improper Selection of Grand Jury must be filed pretrial. But a Motion to Dismiss Indictment for Lack of Jurisdiction or for Failure to State an Offense may be filed at any time.

41. To: Judge Neophyte

From: Law Clerk

Re: Motions

Dear Judge,

Motion practice in criminal cases is very different from the practice in civil cases. There are no specific lists of available motions spelled out in the Federal Rules of Criminal Procedure. Criminal system lawyers are generally free to use whatever caption and motion text best serves their needs that adequately states the relief they seek and the grounds for that relief. *See* Rule 47(b).

With that being said, it would be impossible to prepare a short list of the exact motions that you will be asked to rule on because such a list would be bounded only by the creativity of the local bar. In general, however, you can expect exclusionary motions (to exclude confessions, evidence from searches, etc.), motions to admit evidence, bail motions, motions to modify or dismiss indictments, motions to compel or limit discovery, motions for the government to pay for expert and investigatory services for indigent defendants, and, most frequently, motions for a continuance. You can also expect many motions that embrace several or none of these broad categories.

42. One option, of course, is to spend the weekend preparing to argue against the Motion to Suppress. This would please the judge but could compromise your case if you are unable to prepare adequately over the weekend.

Another option is to request a total continuance or at least a continuance of the hearing on the confession issue. This would give you time to prepare your response to the new motion, but might well anger the judge who does not like continuances. Under this second option, you would have to present the judge with the facts and convince him or her that you were not in any way at fault in needing more time to respond to the Motion to Suppress. Perhaps the judge would need to know that your case could be seriously weakened if the confession were suppressed. You might also suggest that the defense counsel was at fault in not preparing and submitting the Motion in time for you to prepare to meet it. You should also tell the court how long a continuance you request and why this period of time is needed.

43. **Answer (C) is correct.** A motion in limine is a pre-trial motion that allows the court fully to adjudicate likely "hot button" issues at trial. Since this motion is filed and may be resolved before trial, both parties are on notice about the court's ruling on the issue and, if the ruling excludes the evidence, may be required to instruct their witnesses that they may not talk about the excluded issue.

Answer (A) is incorrect. This approach might not work because even the most attentive lawyer may not rise to object before the opposing party or a witness begins to discuss a sensitive topic in front of the jury. Also, you would like to know in advance of trial whether any of the previous incidents is admissible. This information may shed new light on whether you should consider any outstanding plea offers as well as to plan how you will handle such devastating evidence.

Answer (B) is incorrect because the prior incidents may well be brought up by prosecution witnesses, such as the investigating officer, on direct examination. Accordingly, defense counsel's efforts to avoid such questions will not necessarily prevent the issue from being raised.

Answer (D) is incorrect because such questions of law are ultimately for the court to decide and you have a duty to zealously defend your client and bring to the court's attention any tactically wise motion that could assist your client and is ethically permissible. Perhaps the prior incidents could be excluded under an evidence rule as being unfairly prejudicial in the case (see Federal Rule of Evidence 403).

44. **Answer (A) is correct.** The movant, in this case the trial-level defense attorney, has the duty not only to file a motion but also to ensure that the court acts on it (or at least formally request such action, with the request and judge's response on the record for appellate consideration). In reality, a defendant may file many motions, some of which may be overlooked or ignored by the court. Therefore, a party must bring to the court's attention any motion that it would like the court to resolve. Appellate courts generally will not rule on matters not originally resolved by the trial judge.

Answer (B) is incorrect because there is no reversible error in this case on the part of the trial court. Each party must see to it that its motions are heard and a decision reached.

Answer (C) is incorrect because the issue was probably waived when it was not taken up originally in the trial court. However, an appellate court could very well order this in the interests of fundamental fairness or upon a showing of ineffective assistance of counsel at trial. The appellate court could also deem it "plain error" under Federal Rule of Criminal Procedure 52(b) and consider the issue despite trial counsel's failure to request a ruling on the unresolved motion.

Answer (D) is incorrect because an appellate court in virtually all instances will not consider an issue until it is fully adjudicated at the trial court level. Of course, the court could consider it under plain error, as described above.

45. **Answer (D) is correct.** Obviously, the outcome in such a situation may vary somewhat between jurisdictions and individual courts. However, in the absence of a local rule to the contrary, under the Federal Rules of Criminal Procedure (which are silent on the issue), prosecutors are generally free to offer only oral responses (or even no responses) to defense motions. Given a typical prosecutor's large caseload, many do not respond in writing to every filed motion when most defendants will end up pleading guilty anyway. Naturally, some trial courts in certain cases will encourage and even require written responses in especially complex matters. Moreover, in some locales, especially federal court, the practice is that there is a written response to each motion filed by adversary counsel.

Answer (A) is incorrect because the Federal Rules of Criminal Procedure do not restrict the type of response required for each written motion. Again, a local judge or the local court rules may impose such restrictions but the Federal Rules of Criminal Procedure do not.

Answer (B) is incorrect because not required by the Federal Rules of Criminal Procedure, though the trial court does have the inherent authority to grant a continuance and order a written response to all or certain defense motions. Once again, local rules may require such responses unless excused by the court.

Answer (C) is also incorrect because the Federal Rules of Criminal Procedure impose no requirement to file a timely written objection to a motion. Again, local court rules may require a written response to all or certain motions and may even bar an oral response by the government if there was an unreasonable failure to file a written response.

46. Under Federal Rule of Criminal Procedure 29, a Motion for Judgment of Acquittal (formerly known as a motion for directed verdict) may be made virtually any time during the trial. Rule 29 states that it may be made after the evidence for either side is closed, after the jury returns a guilty verdict or is discharged without having returned a verdict, or even within 14 days after the jury is discharged or a guilty verdict is rendered.

Rule 29(b) gives the judge significant latitude in when there must be a ruling on a Motion for Judgment of Acquittal. The issue is whether the evidence is insufficient to sustain a conviction. Rule 29(a). The court may rule on the Motion when it is made or may reserve decision until before the jury returns a verdict. The judge also has the option of resolving the Motion after the jury returns a verdict of guilty or is discharged without having returned the verdict.

47. **Answer (B) is correct.** Under Rule 29(d), a court entering a Judgment of Acquittal after a jury verdict of guilty must conditionally determine whether a motion for new trial should be granted if the appellate court reverses the trial court's decision granting the Motion for Judgment of Acquittal.

Answer (A) is incorrect. Rule 29 specifically authorizes appellate review of a Motion for Judgment of Acquittal granted after a jury verdict of guilty.

Answer (C) is incorrect. Rule 29(d)(2) specifically provides that a conditional grant of a motion for new trial does not affect the finality of the judgment of acquittal.

Answer (D) is incorrect. Rule 29(d) implicitly authorizes the government to appeal a trial court's granting of a Motion for Judgment of Acquittal. The Double Jeopardy Clause does not bar this appeal since, if successful, the original conviction is simply restored and no second trial will be held.

48. **Answer (C) is correct.** Rule 33(a) specifically authorizes the trial judge to vacate a conviction and grant a new trial "if the interest of justice so requires."

Answers (A), (B), and (D) are incorrect. Although the violations listed in Answers (A), (B), and (D) may well convince a court to vacate a judgment "in the interest of justice," those answers do not correctly describe the vague standard adopted in Rule 33(a).

49. **Answer (C) is correct.** Federal Rule of Criminal Procedure 33(b) establishes two specific time limits for filing a Motion for New Trial. If the Motion is based on newly discovered evidence, as in the above question, the Motion must be filed within three years after the verdict or finding of guilty.

Answers (A), (B), and (D) are incorrect because they misstate Rule 33(b)'s three-year limit for newly discovered evidence. It should be noted that Rule 33(b) sets a far shorter time limit for filing a Motion for New Trial for reasons other than newly discovered evidence. For these other grounds, the Motion must be filed within 14 days after the verdict or finding of guilty.

50. The Motion for Judgment of Acquittal (Rule 29) is granted when the evidence at trial was insufficient to sustain the conviction. Thus, it involves ending a trial before verdict or second-guessing the jury's decision after a guilty verdict is given.

The Motion for a New Trial (Rule 33) is permitted "if the interest of justice so requires." The grounds are open-ended, but specifically include newly discovered evidence.

The Motion in Arrest of Judgment (Rule 34), which itself is rarely sought or granted, narrowly authorizes a judgment to be "arrested" (1) if the indictment or information does not charge an offense or (2) if the court does not have jurisdiction over the crime.

51. Your client has a Sixth Amendment right to have "compulsory process for obtaining witnesses in his favor." While this right is subject to reasonable limits, Judge Weerde's "extraordinary need" standard probably violates it in the context of your complex case. *Washington v. Texas*, 388 U.S. 14 (1967), and other Supreme Court cases, provide that an accused has a right to present witnesses to establish a defense. In *Washington*, the defendant was unconstitutionally denied the right to call a codefendant as a witness who would testify that the defendant was not present when the fatal shot was fired. Judge Weerde's restrictive approach may well result in your client being unable to present a full defense, in violation of both the Sixth Amendment and due process. *See also Taylor v. Illinois*, 484 U.S. 400 (1988) (competing considerations in remedy for discovery violation).

52. **Answer (C) is correct.** Under Rule 17(a) of the Federal Rules of Criminal Procedure, a subpoena is issued by the court clerk, under the seal of the court.

    Answers (A) and (B) are incorrect. A judge or prosecutor may also order a subpoena from the court clerk, but, once again, the subpoena is actually issued by the court clerk as part of the clerk's administrative duties.

    Answer (D) is incorrect. Even though the prosecutor or judge may have the subpoena served on this new witness, the subpoena is still *issued* by the court clerk.

53. **Answer (C) is correct.** Under Federal Rule of Criminal Procedure 17(a), the clerk must issue the subpoena in blank. Defense counsel will fill in the name of the person subpoenaed and the clerk's office would not have a record of that name.

    Answer (A) is not the best choice since defense counsel may have a subpoena issued in blank which will protect the identity of the witness who is subpoenaed.

    Answers (B) and (D) are incorrect because the clerk's office does not maintain a record of the people who are subpoenaed. The subpoenas are issued in blank.

54.   **Answer (C) is correct.** Under Federal Rule of Criminal Procedure 25, if a judge becomes disabled during a federal trial, another judge may proceed with the trial upon certifying "familiarity with the trial record."

           Answers (A) and (B) are incorrect because the trial may continue with or without the consent of the lawyers or the accused.

           Answer (D) is incorrect because Rule 25 specifically permits the rest of the trial to be conducted by a substitute judge.

55.   **Answer (A) is correct.** Under Rule 25(b) of the Federal Rules of Criminal Procedure, after a defendant is found guilty, another regularly sitting judge may handle the remaining judicial responsibilities in the case if the judge who presided in the trial is absent, dead, or otherwise disabled.

           Answer (B) is incorrect since under Rule 25(b), a new judge may complete the sentencing part of the trial even though he or she did not preside over the trial.

           Answer (C) is incorrect. Judge Al-Haftiri does not have to handle the sentencing; another judge may do so under Rule 25(b) if Judge Al-Haftiri is disabled and cannot hold a sentencing hearing.

           Answer (D) is incorrect. Rule 25 does not authorize the accused to decide whether the original judge or a new judge would preside over the sentencing hearing.

56. A criminally accused person may want to plead no contest (also called a *nolo contendere* plea) to avoid prejudice in a subsequent civil or criminal case. The no contest plea does not affect the sentence in the instant criminal case since it has the same effect as a guilty plea. The primary advantage of a no contest plea is that in most jurisdictions such a plea or the resulting conviction would not be admissible in a later civil or criminal case to prove liability. Federal Rules of Evidence 410 and 803(22).

In this case, a *nolo* plea in the criminal case may be helpful in the later civil wrongful death case by not providing at least some evidence that the defendant was drunk at the time of the collision.

Some states do not allow *nolo contendere* pleas at all and the rest give the judge broad discretion in agreeing to accept or reject a *nolo contendere* plea.

57. **Answer (D) is correct** because Rule 11(f) provides that "[t]he admissibility or inadmissibility of a plea, a plea discussion, and any related statement is governed by Federal Rule of Evidence 410," which renders a *nolo contendere* inadmissible in a subsequent trial but may admit an accepted plea of guilty as evidence.

Answer (A) is incorrect because, in order to withdraw either a guilty plea or *nolo contendere* plea after the court accepts the plea but before sentencing, the defendant is required to "show a fair and just reason for requesting the withdrawal" pursuant to Rule 11(d)(2)(B).

Answer (B) is incorrect because Rule 11(b)(2) states "[b]efore accepting a plea of guilty or *nolo contendere*, the court must address the defendant personally in open court and determine that the plea is voluntary and did not result from force, threats, or promises (other than promises in a plea agreement)."

Answer (C) is incorrect because Rule 11(c)(1) states "[t]he court must not participate in [plea agreement] discussions." Thus, the court cannot advise the defendant whether to negotiate a *nolo contendere* plea during plea negotiations. Some states do allow the trial judge to participate in plea discussions.

58. **Answer (B) is correct.** This plea, the product of an agreement on a specific maximum sentence, is governed by Rule 11(c)(1)(C). Under Federal Rules of Criminal Procedure 11(c)(3)(A) and 11(c)(5), the court may accept or reject this plea agreement. However, it may not accept the guilty plea but then reject the plea agreement that induced the plea. Under Rule 11(d)(2)(A), Kimberly is free to withdraw her guilty plea if any part of the plea agreement is disapproved by the court. Moreover, such a withdrawal of a guilty plea is generally not admissible in any civil or criminal court. Federal Rule of Criminal Procedure 11(f) indicates that the admissibility of a plea is determined by Federal Rule of Evidence 410, which makes it clear that a withdrawn guilty plea is inadmissible, against the defendant who made the plea, in any civil or criminal proceeding.

Answer (A) is incorrect because it indicates incorrectly, that the attempted guilty plea is admissible.

Answer (C) is incorrect because the plea may be withdrawn if the plea agreement is not accepted by the court.

Answer (D) is incorrect because trial judges do not have to accept any plea agreement. But if a court rejects a plea agreement of the type offered Kimberly, it must allow the accused to withdraw the plea made pursuant to the rejected agreement.

59.   **Answer (A) is correct.** The general rule is that the prosecution must live up to its plea agreements. *Santobello v. New York*, 404 U.S. 257 (1971). If David fully adhered to his end of the bargain, the prosecutor must live up to her part. Since the facts in this hypothetical do not indicate clearly whether or not David gave "truthful testimony" as required in the plea agreement, the court should make a factual inquiry to resolve the issue. If David did satisfy his responsibilities, the prosecutor must recommend the lower sentence or, if the prosecutor refuses to do so, the court must sentence David to the lower term.

Answer (B) is incorrect because plea agreements are generally viewed as contractual-type arrangements. If David met his duties under the plea agreement, the prosecutor must meet hers.

Answer (C) is incorrect because courts can and often do inquire into the nature of a plea agreement and interpret it if need be. The court can also reject an offered plea agreement. A court, however, normally cannot become a part of the plea negotiation process. Federal Rules of Criminal Procedure 11(c)(1) (the court must not participate in plea agreement discussions).

Answer (D) is incorrect because it is not clear whether the prosecutor lived up to the letter of the plea agreement. Moreover, even if the prosecution violated the agreement, the remedy is not dismissal of the case. It would be either enforcement of the agreement or allowing David to withdraw his plea. However, if David has already complied fully with his part of the deal, the remedy of specific performance may be most appropriate.

60.   **Answer (C) is correct.** The United States Supreme Court has held there is no constitutional prohibition against having criminal defendants who face a jury serve longer prison sentences. *Brady v. U.S.*, 397 U.S. 742 (1970). The *Brady* Court reasoned that the plea is still voluntary despite the pressure posed by a possible longer sentence if the accused chooses to have a trial rather than plead guilty. This plea is advantageous to both the government and the defendant. The government gets a more timely resolution of the case, perhaps better serving the goals of punishment, reduces its vulnerability to a bad trial result, and saves considerable resources. The accused gets a more lenient sentence, reduces the risk of a higher sentence, and, according to *Brady*, "demonstrates by his plea that he is ready and willing to admit his crime and to enter the correctional system in a frame of mind that affords hope for success in rehabilitation over a shorter period of time than might otherwise be necessary."

Answer (A) is therefore incorrect.

Answers (B) and (D) are incorrect. *Brady* specifically held that the possibility of a lower sentence does not make a plea involuntary. Accordingly, the Constitution does not bar a differential in sentence for those who plead and those who go to trial.

61. **Answer (D) is correct.** Courts have long recognized that co-conspirators do not necessarily have to be convicted of consistent verdicts or outcomes. In this case, Sarah voluntarily made a fair bargain that avoided any possibility of a long prison sentence. She will, therefore, be held to the bargain she made regardless of how other trials come out.

Answer (A) is incorrect because inconsistent convictions are allowable.

Answer (B) is incorrect because the fundamental fairness doctrine would not apply here. Sarah voluntarily entered a plea to avoid the risk of a harsh sentence. Fundamental fairness was not violated.

Answer (C) is incorrect because the plea bargain process does not require knowledge of the ultimate result of all proceedings. All it requires is that the plea was made knowingly, intelligently, and voluntarily under the circumstances.

62. **Answer (B) is correct.** In general, to date defense counsel have been under no Sixth Amendment obligation to inform their clients of the "collateral consequences" of conviction. However, in *Padilla v. Kentucky*, 559 U.S. 356 (2010), the Court held that defense counsel's failure to apprise a client of the adverse immigration-related consequences of a guilty plea (automatic deportation) constituted ineffective assistance of counsel under *Strickland v. Washington*, 466 U.S. 668 (1984). The *Padilla* Court, however, was at pains to emphasize the particularly significant personal consequences of deportation; loss of the right to vote, while of course significant, would not likely be deemed so significant as to warrant relief.

Answer (A) is incorrect because a lawyer should advise a client about all foreseeable consequences before recommending a course of action, regardless of whether they have anything to do with sentencing. Jack's ignorance of this law, by itself, will not bar his efforts to allege his lawyer should have informed him about the new law.

Answer (C) is incorrect because a court is not obligated to inform the defendant of every negative consequence of a guilty plea. Federal Rule of Criminal Procedure 11(b) provides a list of topics the court must address with the defendant. The voting disenfranchisement law is not included in that list. That is the job of the defense attorney. The court is required to inform the defendant only about the most noteworthy rights that he or she gives up when pleading guilty.

Answer (D) is incorrect because a criminal defense lawyer should apprise his or her clients about laws that will markedly affect the lives of their clients who plead guilty. Failure to do so, however, will not automatically establish ineffective assistance of counsel, as noted in the explanation of Answer (A) above.

63. In *Missouri v. Frye*, 132 S. Ct. 1399 (2012), the Supreme Court held that in assessing whether a criminal accused was accorded the Sixth Amendment's effective assistance of counsel in the context of pleas, the proper standard is that of *Strickland v. Washington*, 466 U.S. 668 (1984). *Strickland* found a two-prong test must be met in order to prove an ineffective assistance case: (1) counsel's performance must be ineffective (*i.e.*, deficient), and (2) the ineffectiveness must have prejudiced the accused.

Frye held that the first prong, ineffective performance, requires defense counsel, in general, "to communicate formal offers from the prosecution to accept a plea on terms and conditions that may be favorable to the accused." Since counsel never communicated the offer to Marilyn, the first prong of *Strickland* is satisfied.

The second prong, a showing of prejudice, means the defendant must establish "a reasonable probability that the end result of the criminal process would have been more favorable by reason of a plea to a lesser charge or a sentence of less prison time." This means the defendant must establish a reasonable probability that she would have accepted the earlier plea offer had it been communicated and that this plea offer would not have been withdrawn by the prosecutor or rejected by the court.

In the instant case, Marilyn likely will lose. The initial offer of three years in prison plus long-term drug testing is not significantly less onerous than the one that she eventually accepted: four years in prison with no drug testing. Since her experienced lawyer reasonably thought a better offer would eventually be forthcoming and would have communicated that to her, it is likely she would not have accepted the initial three-year offer so she may have suffered no prejudice from the lawyer's wrongful failure to apprise her of it.

64.   **Answer (A) is correct.** While *Missouri v. Frye*, 132 S. Ct. 1399 (2012), held that in some circumstances bad advice by defense counsel in a criminal case may offend the Sixth Amendment, this is not likely the case with Marilyn. To prove ineffective assistance in the context of plea bargains, the defendant must establish that counsel's performance fell below that of a reasonably competent defense lawyer and that the performance was prejudicial.

In the instant case, defense counsel did not perform below the level required under the Sixth Amendment. Counsel accurately (as far as we know) advised Marilyn of the likelihood that a better deal would be forthcoming and could not have anticipated the subsequent change in policy. Indeed, had counsel not advised Marilyn of the likely better deal, she could have argued ineffective assistance for not so informing her! Thus, it is likely Marilyn's claim will be denied because her counsel did not perform below that required by the Sixth Amendment.

Answer (B) is incorrect because the fact that she did have a fair trial does not mean her Sixth Amendment rights were not violated by counsel's pretrial performance. *See Frye, supra.*

Answer (C) is incorrect because the Sixth Amendment does not impose strict liability on defense counsel. Advice must be professionally competent; it does not have to be perfect.

Answer (D) is incorrect because the actual outcome is irrelevant under the Sixth Amendment if counsel performed at a constitutionally acceptable level. Though Marilyn is certainly unhappy with the result, her Sixth Amendment rights were not violated by counsel's competent advice and a later shift in policy by the government.

65.   **Answer (D) is correct.** Despite the harsh result, the United States Supreme Court has held that prosecutors have virtually unfettered discretion to pursue any charges they choose to pursue. *See Bordenkircher v. Hayes*, 434 U.S. 357 (1978). The theory is that the trial court and the jury serve as a vital check on this authority and may refuse to convict or may convict on lesser charges if they so choose. Although a prosecutor has a great deal of power over what charges are brought, the defendant is protected because the prosecutor must still obtain a conviction and the court must follow the law in setting the sentence. Both the trial and sentence may be challenged on appeal. Details of the plea bargaining process are

generally irrelevant to appellate courts reviewing a particular case where no plea was entered and the case was resolved by a trial.

Answers (A) and (C) are therefore incorrect.

Answer (B) is incorrect because there is no legal ground to overturn the sentence and allow Kenny the opportunity to accept the original two-year offer. Kenny had a chance to do so and turned it down. The prosecutor's decision to seek a three-strike sentence was within his or her discretion even though the prosecutor's motives are less than admirable.

66.   **Answer (A) is correct** (it expresses an inaccurate standard). If the trial court has not yet accepted Annette's plea, under Rule 11(d)(1) she may withdraw it "for any reason or no reason." Thus, the standard of "a substantial reason that serves the interests of justice" is too high and incorrect.

Answer (B) is incorrect (because it expresses an accurate standard). Under Rule 11(d)(2)(A), if the plea is accepted but sentence has not yet been imposed, the defendant may withdraw the plea if the court rejects the agreement for a two-year maximum sentence in exchange for a guilty plea.

Answer (C) is incorrect (because it expresses an accurate standard). Under Rule 11(d)(2)(B), if the plea is accepted but sentence has not been imposed, the defendant may withdraw the plea if the defendant can show a "fair and just reason for requesting the withdrawal."

Answer (D) is incorrect (because it expresses an accurate standard). Under Rule 11(e), after the court accepts a plea and imposes sentence, the defendant may not withdraw the plea. He or she may only have it set aside on direct appeal or collateral attack.

67.   Your client is seeking to enter an *Alford* or "best-interests" plea. According to the Supreme Court in *North Carolina v. Alford*, 400 U.S. 25 (1970), the judge has the discretion to accept or reject this type of plea. As long as the plea is knowing and voluntary, the Constitution and Rule 11 are satisfied, despite the defendant's claim of innocence.

If the plea is rejected, the court should schedule a trial to decide whether the defendant is guilty or innocent. If the court accepts the plea, the judge could follow Rule 11, particularly with regard to establishing a factual basis for the plea.

68.   In a minority of American courts, such as that in the question, a defendant will have to either plead guilty and admit to the crime under oath or go to trial. In these locales a defendant may not plead guilty and deny guilt at the same time. Your client is not compelled to incriminate himself in violation of the Fifth Amendment because he may remain silent and have a trial fair trial that fully satisfies the Constitution.

States are free to set their own requirements for permitting a trial court to accept a guilty plea, including the requirement to waive the Fifth Amendment and admit guilt. There is no federal constitutional right to enter an *Alford* or "best interests" plea where the defendant pleads guilty but denies being guilty. *See North Carolina v. Alford*, 400 U.S. 25 (1970). Your client has a tough choice, but one of them is to assert his Fifth Amendment rights not to incriminate himself.

69.   **Answer (C) is correct.** Dora wants to enter an *Alford* or "best interests" plea. This plea was approved by the United States Supreme Court in *North Carolina v. Alford*, 400 U.S. 25

(1970). Though the defendant denies guilt, the plea is a guilty plea and authorizes the court to impose sentence as with any other guilty plea.

Answer (A) is incorrect because an *Alford* plea leads to a conviction that may be admissible later.

Answer (B) is incorrect. A defendant whose *Alford* plea is accepted by the court is convicted, and the plea has the same effect and consequences as any other kind of guilty plea.

Answer (D) is incorrect because an *Alford* plea is not a no contest or *nolo contendere* plea. The *Alford* plea is a guilty plea.

70. **Answer (A) is correct.** The rule of *caveat emptor* applies (let the buyer beware). The prosecutor should never have offered a deal not knowing whether the children were dead or alive. Viktor appears to have complied fully with his part of the bargain.

Answer (B) is incorrect because of the vague "offer" Viktor was not required to indicate whether the victims were living or deceased. Viktor accepted the offer that was put on the table and there is no indication of bad faith by Viktor. Indeed, the prosecutor may have made the offer to get the case resolved and the families some peace, irrespective whether the children were dead or alive.

Answer (C) is incorrect because there is a valid offer and acceptance, the necessary elements of a plea deal.

Answer (D) is incorrect. Even though the deal had not been accepted by the court, the defendant fully complied with his part of the deal and the government must as well.

71. **Answer (C) is correct.** A plea entered in federal court will be valid if it complies with Federal Criminal Procedure Rule 11 and other federal law. There is no independent legal significance to the particular script a court chooses to use. Conversely, the plea entry is not necessarily insulated from future challenge even if a script approved by local lawyers and judges is used verbatim. Furthermore, a plea entry may be valid even if the wrong script or no script is used. The key is whether the rules of criminal procedure are actually followed.

Answer (A) is incorrect. No statute is needed for a federal district to establish a method of handling pleas under Rule 11. The only requirement is that whatever script is used complies with Rule 11 and other applicable laws.

Answer (B) is incorrect because the proceeding using the new script may have involved reversible error in the text of the unapproved script. The question contains no facts indicating whether or not the error was harmless and so this answer is incorrect without more information.

Answer (D) is incorrect. Rule 11 dictates what rights and other matters the court must inform the defendant about, but does not mandate that the rule itself be read to the accused. The point is that the defendant must be told of the substance of the rules but not the actual wording of the rule itself.

72. **Answer (C) is correct.** A guilty plea does not waive the defendant's Sixth Amendment right to the effective assistance of counsel. He or she has this right during the plea process and can appeal the denial of the right to the effective assistance of counsel during plea proceedings.

Answers (A), (B), and (D) are incorrect. A guilty plea, however, routinely involves a waiver of jury trial (Answer (A)), confrontation (Answer (B)), and self-incrimination (Answer (D)). *See* Federal Rule of Criminal Procedure 11(b)(1). The accused should be apprised of each as part of the plea process.

73. **Answer (D) is correct.** Rule 11 of the Federal Rules of Criminal Procedure does not mention a reserved plea as an option, although some federal courts use their inherent authority and permit defendants to reserve the plea. This essentially postpones the entry of the plea until a later date, perhaps to allow plea bargaining between the defense counsel and the prosecutors. If the accused who reserved a plea later chooses to enter one, he or she must choose between those authorized by Rule 11(a)(1).

    Answers (A), (B), and (C) are incorrect. Rule 11(a)(1) specifically authorizes a guilty plea (Answer (A)), not guilty plea (Answer (B)), and *nolo contendere* plea (Answer (C)).

74. **Answer (C) is correct.** Under Rule 11(a)(2) of the Federal Rules of Criminal Procedure, an accused may enter a conditional guilty plea, reserving the right to appeal an adverse determination by the trial court. The court and government must consent to this.

    Answer (A) is incorrect because the guilty plea effectively waives the confession issue, rendering it highly unlikely the appellate court would reverse on this ground.

    Answer (B) is incorrect because it deprives Bert of the favorable plea offer and exposes him to a potential sentence far harsher than that offered in plea negotiations.

    Answer (D) is incorrect because it deprives the accused of the possibility that an appellate court will suppress the confession. If the confession is ruled inadmissible, Bert could possibly have the charges dropped, win an acquittal at trial, or at least get an especially favorable plea deal from a prosecutor who has lost the use of critical evidence.

75. **Answer (C) is correct** (*i.e.*, it is not true). The issue need not be so critical that any conviction would be reversed if the defendant prevails on appeal. Rule 11(a)(2) does not deal with how significant the issue to be appealed must be.

    Answers (A), (B), and (D) are all incorrect because they are all specifically required by Rule 11(a)(2)'s authorization of a conditional plea.

76. **Answer (A) is correct.** Under Rule 11 of the Federal Rules of Criminal Procedure, the court has many obligations during plea proceedings. Answer (A) is correct, however, since the court does not have to ensure that defense counsel thoroughly worked up the case.

    Answer (B) is incorrect because the court must ensure that the plea is voluntary. Rule 11(b)(2).

    Answer (C) is incorrect because the court must ensure that there is a factual basis for the plea. Rule 11(b)(3).

    Answer (D) is incorrect because the court must inform the defendant of the maximum possible penalty, even if the maximum exceeds that agreed on by the parties as part of the plea deal. Rule 11(b)(1)(H).

77. **Answer (C) is correct.** Under Federal Criminal Procedure Rule 11(a)(2), the government must consent if the accused is to be permitted to enter a conditional plea.

Answers (A), (B), and (D) are incorrect because, under Rule 11(a)(1), the accused may enter a guilty, not guilty, or *nolo contendere* plea irrespective of the presence of absence of the government's consent. The court, though not the prosecuting attorney, must consent before a nolo plea is entered. Rule 11(a)(1).

78.   A criminal accused who pleads guilty waives many important constitutional rights. These rights are outlined in Federal Rule of Criminal Procedure 11(b), which requires that the accused be apprised of the rights waived by the plea.

    The rights that are waived by the guilty plea include the rights to: plead not guilty, have a trial, impanel a jury for that trial, be represented by effective counsel at the trial and at every other stage of the proceedings, confront and cross-examine adverse witnesses, issue compulsory process to obtain witnesses at a trial, assert a Fifth Amendment right not to be compelled to testify at trial, testify in his or her own defense, and present evidence at a trial.

79. To: Boss

From: Law Clerk 1

1. Failure to satisfy Rule 12.2 of the Federal Rules of Criminal Procedure may bar us from raising the insanity defense.

2. To satisfy Rule 12.2, at the time for filing pretrial motions (unless this deadline is changed by the court), we must notify the prosecutor in writing (with a copy filed with the court clerk) of our intention to rely upon an insanity defense. Rule 12.2(a).

3. Similarly, if we plan on using expert testimony relating to a mental condition bearing upon guilt, we must also provide notice similar to that outlined above. Rule 12.2(b).

4. After this notice is filed, if the government so moves, the court may order our client to be examined by certain mental health professionals. Rule 12.2(c). Our client must submit to the exam or we may be barred from introducing our own expert testimony on our client's mental status. Rule 12.2(d). Although this procedure will subject our client to a mental evaluation that might not support an insanity defense, the process has the advantage of providing us with a free mental evaluation. The expert conducting the evaluation may not testify about any statements made by the defendant during the examination, except on an issue concerning mental status on which our client has introduced expert testimony. *Kansas v. Cheever*, 134 S. Ct. 596 (2013).

5. If we change our mind and withdraw either the notice to use an insanity defense or the notice to use expert testimony, the notice we originally gave is not admissible against our client. Rule 12.2(e).

80. **Answer (D) is correct.** Rule 12.1 does not require the government to show the defense its entire investigative file whenever the defense offers an alibi defense. Of course, under *Brady v. Maryland*, 373 U.S. 83 (1963), the prosecution must provide the defense with information about witnesses who will support the alibi defense.

Answer (A) is incorrect (because it is an accurate statement of the law). Rule 12.1(a)(1) requires that the government request in writing notice of the defendant's intent to present an alibi defense.

Answer (B) is incorrect (because it is an accurate statement of the law). Rule 12.1(a)(1) states that the government's request for notice of an alibi defense must include a statement of the time, date, and place of the homicide.

Answer (C) is incorrect (because it is an accurate statement of the law). Rule 12.1(b)(1) requires the government, after the defense has provided notice of an intent to use an alibi defense, to inform the defendant of the names, address, and telephone number of government witnesses, other than the victim, to be called to establish the defendant's presence at the homicide.

81.   **Answer (A) is correct.** Rule 12.1 does not require the accused to present an affidavit under oath swearing the alibi defense is offered in good faith.

    Answers (B), (C), and (D) are incorrect because Rule 12.1(a)(2) mandates that the defense give the prosecution notice of an intent to offer an alibi defense (Answer B), the location where the defendant claims to have been (C), and the names and addresses, etc. of each alibi witness the defense intends to call (D).

82.   **Answer (B) is correct.** One of the primary reasons for disclosure in both rules is to prevent surprises and surprise tactics at trial. Also, both Rules 12.1(f) and 12.2(e) prevent the admissibility of a withdrawn notice against the party withdrawing it.

    Answer (A) is incorrect. Rule 12.2 on the insanity defense is initiated by the defense, while Rule 12.1 is initiated by the prosecution.

    Answer (C) is incorrect. Choice III is not required by either rule since possible witnesses contacted about the alibi or insanity defense need not be disclosed. Disclosure is limited to alibi witnesses and insanity experts to be used by the parties.

    Answer (D) is incorrect. Choices (I) and (IV) are correct, rendering answer (D) incorrect.

83.   The failure to comply with Rule 12.1, notice of alibi defense, depends on which side did not comply and at what stage the noncompliance occurred. Since Rule 12.1 is triggered by a government written request for notice of an intent to offer an alibi defense, if the government fails to make the request, the defense is not obligated to provide alibi information in advance of trial. If the defense fails to respond adequately to the government request, under Rule 12.1 it is not entitled to have the government disclose the names and addresses of its own location witnesses. Similarly, if either party does not comply with its obligations under Rule 12.1, the court is authorized to exclude the testimony of the undisclosed witness.

    For Rule 12.2, if the defendant fails to provide notice of an intent to use a mental health expert under Rule 12.2(a) or to submit to an examination under 12.2(c), the court may exclude expert evidence on the issue of the defendant's mental disability and may even exclude an insanity defense itself if there is a failure to notify of an intent to present this defense.

84. **Answer (D) is correct.** Even though Jeremy may well have lost a chance to prove his innocence, the case will not be dismissed. Under *Arizona v. Youngblood*, 488 U.S. 51 (1988), due process does not require the police to preserve all evidence in a criminal case. Answer (D) is correct because *Youngblood* held that unless "a criminal defendant can show bad faith on the part of the police, failure to preserve potentially useful evidence does not constitute a denial of due process of law."

    Answers (A) and (B) are incorrect. The police have no duty to preserve all relevant evidence. They may destroy evidence even if it compromises the defendant's possible defense as long as they do not act in bad faith.

    Answer (C) is incorrect. Police bad faith is the key; therefore Answer (C) is not the best answer. The speculative possibility that the evidence may have assisted the defendant is not dispositive since this uncertainty may be present irrespective of good or bad faith actions by the police. *Brady* is not dispositive since the destroyed materials provided no information helpful to either side. Accordingly, the destroyed evidence was not helpful to the accused and was not covered by *Brady v. Maryland*, 373 U.S. 83 (1963).

85. You should turn this over to the defense for two reasons. First, in *Brady v. Maryland*, 373 U.S. 83 (1963), the United States Supreme Court held that due process requires the government to give the accused any evidence, favorable to the accused on guilt or punishment, that is in the government's possession. Although it is unclear whether this evidence will actually help the defense since it may well be inadmissible (problems with hearsay, lack of personal knowledge, and authentication), the safe course is to give the evidence to the defense and let defense counsel decide whether and how to use it. Perhaps defense counsel will be able to identify the handwriting on the note and then locate the anonymous author. Failure to disclose the document could lead to appellate reversal if the defendant is convicted. *See U.S. v. Bagley*, 473 U.S. 667 (1985).

    The second reason for giving the document to the defense is Federal Rule of Criminal Procedure 16(a)(1)(E), which mandates government disclosure of "documents" that are in the government's possession and are material to preparing the defense. Since the defense has made a formal request under Rule 16 for this kind of evidence, the better course is for the government to assume that somehow this strange document may be material to the preparation of the defense and therefore to disclose it to defense counsel.

86. **Answer (C) is correct.** Rule 16(a)(2) specifically exempts "internal government documents made by an attorney for the government or other government agent in connection with investigating or prosecuting the case" except as specified in the statute.

    Answers (A), (B), and (D) are incorrect because Rule 16 requires the government, upon the defendant's request, to turn over the defendant's oral statements to the police in response to interrogation if the government intends to use them at trial, under Rule

16(a)(1)(A) (Answer (A)); the defendant's prior criminal record, under Rule 16(a)(1)(D) (Answer (B)); and any mental or physical examination of the defendant that the government intends to use at trial, under Rule 16(a)(1)(F) (Answer (D)).

87.   **Answer (B) is correct.** Rule 16 does not mandate pretrial discovery of the substance of oral statements by (non-expert) witnesses.

Answer (A) is incorrect because Rule 16(a)(1)(B) does require the government to give the defense a copy of the defendant's written statement.

Answer (C) is incorrect because Rule 16(a)(1)(D) obligates the prosecution to give the defense a copy of the defendant's criminal record.

Answer (D) is incorrect because Rule 16(a)(1)(E) mandates disclosure of documents within the government's possession which are material to the preparation of the defense.

88.   **Answer (A) is correct.** Rule 16(a)(1)(B) requires the prosecution to turn over written or recorded statements of the defendant, but the Rule does not require the defense to turn over such statements to the prosecution.

Answer (B) is incorrect because Rules 16(a)(1)(F) and 16(b)(1)(B) require exchange of information of examination and tests.

Answer (C) is incorrect because Rules 16(a)(1)(E) and 16(b)(1)(A) mandate mutual disclosure of documents and tangible objects.

Answer (D) is incorrect because Rules 16(a)(1)(G) and 16(b)(1)(C) provide for the exchange of summaries of the testimony of experts intended to be used at trial.

89.   **Answer (C) is correct.** Rule 16(b)(1)(B) requires defense counsel to give the government access to mental evaluations in the reports in the defense files if the defense intends to use the item in its case-in-chief at trial.

Answer (A) is incorrect. Defense counsel need only provide documents that the defense intends to use at trial; the test is not whether it is material to the prosecution's trial preparation.

Answer (B) is incorrect. *Brady v. Maryland* is not reciprocal. Defense counsel need not turn over items merely because the items would be helpful to the prosecution.

Answer (D) is incorrect. When the defense lawyer requests information under Rule 16, he or she effectively waives any objection to providing the government with reciprocal materials that would be detrimental to the defense. You, as defense counsel, can avoid such disclosure by simply not requesting that type of information under Rule 16, which comes into play only upon the "request" by the defense.

90.   **Answer (A) is correct** (*i.e.*, not authorized by Rule 16). Though the trial court is given much discretion in applying sanctions for noncompliance with Rule 16, entering a criminal conviction is not one of them. The accused has a due process right to many procedures before he or she may be convicted. Criminal conviction is not authorized absent compliance with the due process rights.

Answers (B), (C), and (D), are incorrect because they all correctly state a possible remedy specifically permitted by Rule 16(d)(2). Thus, the trial court may grant a continuance

(Answer (B)), prohibit the party from introducing undisclosed evidence (Answer (C)), and enter any "order that is just under the circumstances" (Answer (D)).

91.   **Answer (C) is correct.** Under Rule 12.1(a), notice of alibi processes is begun when the prosecutor makes a written request that the defense notify the government of any intent to use an alibi defense. This request must state the time, date, and place of the alleged offense. Once this request is made, the defense must then inform the prosecution of an intent to use an alibi defense.

        Answer (A) is incorrect because under Rule 12.2(a), the defendant has the responsibility for first informing the prosecution of an intent to rely upon an insanity offense. The prosecution has no such responsibility nor could it since the defense, not the prosecution, would have the information that the defense intends to use an insanity defense.

        Answer (B) is similarly incorrect because Rule 12.2(b) provides that the accused (not the government) must first inform the government of an intent to use expert testimony on the defendant's mental condition bearing upon the issue of guilty.

        Answer (D) is incorrect because Rule 12.3 requires the defendant to first notify the government of an intent to use a defense involving public authority.

92.   **Answer (B) is correct** (*i.e.*, the statement is not accurate). Rule 15(c) specifically provides for the defendant's presence at the deposition. This provision explains why some such depositions are taken at a prison where the defendant is incarcerated. Security concerns may prevent the accused from leaving the prison to attend a deposition conducted elsewhere.

        Answer (A) is incorrect (*i.e.*, the statement is accurate) because under Rule 15(a), a deposition may be ordered only due to "exceptional circumstances" and in the "interest of justice."

        Answer (C) is incorrect (*i.e.*, the statement is accurate). Under Rule 15(a), a deposition in a criminal case is permissible under this provision only if the court so orders. This is a significant difference from depositions in civil cases. Note that nothing in the Federal Rules would prevent the prosecutor and defense counsel from taking the deposition of anyone who consents to being deposed.

        Answer (D) is incorrect (*i.e.*, the statement is accurate) because Rule 15(f) indicates that the deposition may be admissible at trial; indeed, often that is the reason the deposition under Rule 15 is taken.

93.   Your motion will likely be denied. Rule 15 is quite clear that a deposition is available "in order to preserve testimony for trial." Case law makes it clear that this does not mean a "fishing expedition" for discovery. Since your motion does not seem to request the deposition for evidence preservation, it will not be successful under Rule 15.

94.   **Answer (D) is the best answer.** All the previous answers are correct, making Answer (D) the most accurate choice.

        Answer (A) is correct but not the only answer. Rule 15(a)(2) provides that a detained material witness may file a written motion requesting a deposition. Nothing would prevent the government from making this motion on its own.

        Answer (B) is correct but not the only answer. Rule 15(a)(2) provides that a detained material witness must sign under oath a deposition transcript before being released from detention.

Answer (C) is correct but not the only answer. Rule 15(a)(2) provides that a detained material witness may be discharged after being deposed.

95.   **Answer (A) is correct.** Several answers could provide the defense with helpful information, but Answer (A) is the best answer. Under Rule 7(f), the court may direct the prosecutor to file a Bill of Particulars, which will provide the accused with more information about the facts of the case.

Answer (B) is incorrect. The Federal Rules of Criminal Procedure do not authorize requests for admission of facts.

Answer (C) is incorrect because the Federal Rules of Criminal Procedure do not authorize interrogatories in criminal cases.

Answer (D) is not the best answer because depositions are allowed in criminal cases only in "exceptional cases" under Rule 15(a)(1) of the Federal Rules of Criminal Procedure.

96.   **Answer (D) is correct.** Rule 26.2 does not apply in grand jury proceedings. Rule 26.2(g).

Answers (A), (B), and (C) are incorrect. Rule 26.2(g) makes the provision apply in a sentencing hearing (Answer (A)), preliminary hearing (Answer (B)), and suppression hearing (Answer (C)).

97.   **Answer (B) is correct.** Under Rule 26.2(a), the defense is entitled to see statements by a prosecution witness after the witness has testified on direct examination, but only if the defense makes a motion to produce the statement.

Answer (A) is incorrect because the work product doctrine does not protect against disclosure under Rule 26.2.

Answer (C) is incorrect because disclosure does not depend on whether or not the statement appears to be helpful. The defense will make this determination when it decides whether or not to use the statement during cross-examination.

Answer (D) is incorrect because Spotter's wishes are not dispositive. Rule 26(c) does permit the court to excise portions of the statement that contain matters that are privileged or unrelated to the subjects of the direct examination.

98.   The short answer is yes and no. Rule 26.2(a) does apply to statements by the accountant but not to those of the defendant since the latter are specifically excluded.

As far as the information about other illegalities, contained in the accountant's statement, which you do not want disclosed, Rule 26.2 (c) permits you to move the court to redact information in a statement that does not "relate to the subject matter of the witness's testimony." This would be done "in camera" where the judge would inspect the statement without disclosing the contents to the prosecution.

99. Based on the facts in the question, the judge may well deny the motion to compel, though the case is not clear. The decision depends on a balance between the interests of the government, the informant, and the criminal accused. "What is usually referred to as the informer's privilege is in reality the Government's privilege to withhold from disclosure the identity of persons who furnish information of violations of law to officers charged with enforcement of that law." *Roviaro v. U.S.*, 353 U.S. 53, 59 (1957) (citing *Scher v. U.S.*, 305 U.S. 251, 254 (1938)). "The purpose of the privilege is the furtherance and protection of the public interest in effective law enforcement. The privilege recognizes the obligation of citizens to communicate their knowledge of the commission of crimes to law-enforcement officials and, by preserving their anonymity, encourages them to perform that obligation. . . . " *Roviaro v. U.S.*, 353 U.S. at 59. Where the informant and law enforcement purposes would not be harmed by revelation of the informant's identity, the privilege ceases. "A further limitation on the applicability of the privilege arises from the fundamental requirements of fairness. Where the disclosure of an informer's identity . . . is relevant and helpful to the defense of an accused, or is essential to a fair determination of a cause, the privilege must give way." *Roviaro*, 353 U.S. at 60–61.

In this case, the government asserts the informant's very life would be in jeopardy if his or her identity were released, plus future assistance by this informant, still serving in an undercover capacity, would be compromised. The defense could counter with the fact that the defense needs the information to attack the warrant (not based on adequate probable cause) and to help it locate witnesses and discover motives for the prosecution.

On balance, the defense has not offered any compelling need for disclosure of the informant's identity and the prosecution has suggested, though without any proof, that the informant's health and usefulness would be jeopardized by disclosure. Absent more compelling reasons by the defense, disclosure of the informant's identity will likely be denied because of the informant's privilege.

100.   **Answer (D) is the most accurate answer** because prosecution could be held in any of the three jurisdictions.

      Answer (A), which is correct, is not the best answer. The general rule is that criminal court jurisdiction is in the area where the crime occurred. For federal cases, Federal Rule of Criminal Procedure 18 mandates that the prosecution occur in the judicial district where the offense was committed unless a statute or other rule provides otherwise. This would include the federal district court with jurisdiction over federal crimes in Dover County.

      Answers (B) and (C) are also correct, but neither is the best answer. In state systems, the rule that prosecution may occur where the crime occurs means that the prosecution may be in Dover, Albert (or, for that matter, Baker and Carroll Counties as well), since the conspiracy and acts to carry out the conspiracy occurred in all of the four counties.

101.   The general rule is that jurisdiction in a criminal case is where the crime occurred. Here, two states are involved. The State of Truman may try Donald since the initial kidnapping occurred there. The fact that other parts of the ransom scheme were carried out in another state is irrelevant since one element, the seizure of Farnsworth, occurred in Truman and is sufficient to confer jurisdiction in the State of Truman.

      The State of Roosevelt may also have jurisdiction. Many states have adopted a rule that gives a state jurisdiction for a crime either that begins ("commences") or ends ("consummates") in that state or when criminal acts occurred in that state. Here, when Donald took Farnsworth to the State of Roosevelt, venue for the crime, which began in Truman, also occurred in Roosevelt where it ended.

      It should be noted that the separate sovereign doctrine of double jeopardy would permit both states to try Donald for the kidnapping, even though only one person was taken. *See Heath v. Alabama*, 474 U.S. 82 (1985).

102.   **Answer (B) is correct** (*i.e.*, it is not true). Rules 20 and 21 are triggered by a defense motion, not a government one. This is because venue is a right of the defendant who must consent to any change.

      Answer (A) is incorrect (*i.e.*, it is true) since Rule 21 specifically authorizes a venue change to obtain a fair and impartial trial.

      Answer (C) is incorrect (*i.e.*, it is true). Rule 20 specifically permits a defendant's motion to change venue for plea and sentence.

      Answer (D) is incorrect (*i.e.*, it is true) because Rule 20 states that both federal prosecutors must approve in writing a venue change for plea and sentence.

103.   **Answer (A) is correct.** Rule 21 does not mandate the consent of the government as a prerequisite to the court's granting the transfer for convenience. Of course, the court will ordinarily ask the government for its views on the matter. Since the government's consent is not required for a transfer for trial, the procedure for this change differs from that needed for a transfer for plea and sentence in Rule 20, which requires the consent of the United States Attorneys in both districts.

Answer (B) is incorrect (*i.e.*, it is required). A transfer for convenience is given only upon the defendant's motion. Rule 21(b).

Answer (C) is incorrect (*i.e.*, it is required). Rule 21(d) says that the motion for transfer should be filed before arraignment "or at any other time the court or these rules prescribe."

Answer (D) is incorrect. Of course, the court's consent is required since the transfer requires a formal court order.

104. **Answer (A) is correct.** Federal Rule of Criminal Procedure 13 provides that offenses and offenders may be tried together if they could have been joined in an indictment together under Rule 8.

Answer (B) is incorrect because Rule 13 specifically states that offenses that may be joined under Rule 8 may be tried together as well.

Answer (C) is incorrect because under Rule 13, both offenses and offenders may be joined for trial if they could be joined in a single indictment.

Answer (D) is incorrect. Under Rule 8(a) offenses may be joined together but do not have to have occurred at the same time to be so joined. Rule 8(a) permits joinder of offenses that are of the same or similar character, or based on the same act or transaction, or connected with or constitute parts of a common scheme or plan.

105. **Answer (C) is correct.** Under Federal Rule 8(a), joinder of offenses, crimes may be joined together if they are of the "same or similar character, or are based on the same act or transaction, or are connected with or constitute parts of a common scheme or plan." The important thing to remember here is the "common scheme or plan" requirement. Cooter possesses specialized knowledge that he shares with customers and mechanics so they can run their own insurance scams. The illegal dumping is not part of the conspiracies and is not of a similar character to them.

Answer (A) is incorrect because at the very least I and III can be joined.

Answers (B) and (D) are incorrect because defrauding insurance companies and illegal dumping of waste do not meet the Rule 8(a) test. Note that regardless of your answer you should have ignored the language in II, which identifies dumping of hazardous waste products as a misdemeanor. Under Rule 8(a), crimes can be joined together regardless of whether they are felonies (ordinarily defined as crimes punishable by imprisonment for a year or more) or misdemeanors (crimes punishable by imprisonment for less than a year).

106. Under Rule 14(a) of the Federal Rules of Criminal Procedure, the trial court has the discretion to order separate trials on validly joined counts within an indictment or information if it appears that the prosecution or defense would be prejudiced by the joinder. Here the defendant is charged with five homicides and there are strong similarities in them because of the location of the bodies and the fact that all were prostitutes, though much is unknown about some of them. The defendant confessed to killing three of the victims and provided some details about these deaths, but provided no information at all about the other two.

Joinder may be prejudicial in several respects. A jury may find it extremely difficult to consider each individual count on its own set of circumstantial facts. This is unfairly prejudicial to the defendant's right to have a jury find beyond a reasonable doubt that he or she is guilty of each individual count. Thus, if the evidence of guilt for four homicides is quite strong, but that for another one is very weak, the jury may convict of all five without adequate individual consideration of each offense.

The case against joinder is even stronger if, under the Federal Rules of Evidence, evidence of one homicide would be inadmissible in the trial for the others. Joinder would permit the jurors to hear evidence of all homicides even though some of that proof is not to be considered in resolving some of the cases. At the least, this could be quite confusing to jurors and is unlikely to be cured by jury instructions directing the jurors how to use certain evidence.

107.   **Answer (A) is correct.** This question requires an analysis under the joinder of offenses provision of Rule 8(a), Federal Rules of Criminal Procedure. Rule 13 permits a *trial* joinder if Rule 8(a) permits a joinder of *offenses* in an indictment. Rule 8(a) permits joinder of offenses which are of the same or similar character or "based on the same act or transaction" or on "two or more acts . . . connected together or constituting part of a common scheme or plan."

Because the gun in question was found with the defendant who was also in possession of the drugs, this qualifies for joinder under Rule 8(a) since there is a strong connection between possessing a gun and the transportation of illegal drugs. The two are based on the "same act or transaction" and are part of a "common scheme or plan." Drug dealers often carry guns in order to protect their money, drugs, and personal safety. *See U.S. v. Mason*, 658 F.2d 1263 (9th Cir. 1981). If the gun had been found at Raj's home some time later, arguably the two offenses could not be properly joined in one trial. *U.S. v. Terry*, 911 F.2d 272 (9th Cir. 1990).

Answer (B) is incorrect because Federal Rule of Criminal Procedure 8(a) allows joinder of only some offenses, not all offenses with which a person is charged. Answer (B) is too broad to be correct. The criteria of Rule 8(a) must be satisfied before joinder of offenses is permitted.

Answer (C) is incorrect because the court is allowed to consider the entire scheme or transaction or plan, even though the crimes are of a different character.

Answer (D) is incorrect because Rule 8 joinder does not involve discretionary relief from joinder because of prejudice. Rule 14, on the other hand, specifically authorizes relief from prejudicial joinder and would be the proper rule to seek a severance on this ground. Presumably, Raj would still have a chance with a Rule 14 motion.

108.   **Answer (A) is the best answer.** This question requires analysis under Rule 8(b), Federal Rules of Criminal Procedure. Rule 8(b) provides that offenders may be joined together if they participated in the "same act or transaction, or in the same series of acts or transactions." (Rule 8(a) deals with joinder of *offenses* rather than *offenders*.) Rule 8(b) also provides that not all defendants need be charged together in each count of the indictment.

In this case, **Answer (A) is the best answer** because it puts Weisz and Dykstra together possibly discussing obtaining valuable items in exchange for the sewer contract. The various bribery offenses may be part of Rule 8(b)'s "same series of acts or transactions" since the *modus operandi* was so sophisticated and similar. Moreover, the eyewitness may have seen Dykstra and Weisz discussing this particular bribery, rendering it more possible that the bribery of the sewer company by the two public officials was part of the same "series of acts or transactions" under Rule 8(b).

Answer (B) is incorrect because it is insufficient only to show that the two defendants were spoken to by contractors for the sewer project. Presumably, part of their job was to discuss projects with potential contractors. Neither fact is much help to the prosecutor in establishing under Rule 8(b) "the same series of acts or transactions."

Answer (C) is incorrect because providing bail money does not suggest the two were involved in the same act or transaction. They may be just friends.

Answer (D) is not the best answer though it carries a strong suggestion that Weisz and Dykstra might have conspired in getting money for the sewer project. On the other hand, there is no direct evidence linking the two. Similarity in methodology is very weak evidence of the necessary link required by Rule 8(b) to join offenders.

109. **Answer (C) is the best answer.** For Rule 14 prejudicial joinder motions, the movant has the burden of proving prejudice and courts set the bar fairly high. In *Zafiro v. U.S.*, 506 U.S. 534, 539 (1993), the United States Supreme Court described the standard of proof as presented in Answer (C).

Answers (A) and (B) are incorrect because the defendant makes the motion to sever and thus has the burden of proof. Under Rule 14, the trial judge ultimately has a hefty amount of discretion in determining joinder and severance issues.

Answer (D) is not the best answer. The language in Answer (C) is taken from *Zafiro v. U.S.*, 506 U.S. 534, 539 (1993), and is a more accurate choice than the lower "reasonable possibility" standard stated in Answer (D). The difference between Answers (C) and (D) illustrates that severance under Rule 14 requires the movant to make a substantial showing of prejudice. The significant unfavorable evidence about Silva, which is likely not admissible against your client, would be a strong argument in favor of severance since the jury may well condemn your client for associating with someone with such a sordid record.

110. **Answer (C) is the best answer,** though not a strong one. Rule 8(a) requires that for joinder of offenses the charges must be of the "same or similar character," "based on the same act or transaction," or "connected with or constitute parts of a common scheme or plan." Although the court may still deny a severance motion, Answer (C) shows that the bombs, evidencing significant technical differences, might not have been part of some common scheme, though admittedly the argument is not strong. Joinder is very likely in this case.

Answer (A) is incorrect because Rule 8 motions for improper joinder do not hinge on questions of fairness; that is the realm of Rule 14, which authorizes a severance to avoid prejudice to either party.

Answer (B) is a trick answer and not the best answer. The site of mailing is not important if the offenses were of the same or similar character or based on the same act or transaction or part of a common scheme or plan. Rule 8(a). The fact that the bombs were mailed from different locations may well indicate a plan to send the bombs while avoiding apprehension. The offenses may still be part of a common scheme or plan and be of the same character irrespective of the post offices used to send the bombs.

Answer (D) is incorrect because Rule 8 specifically states that felony and misdemeanor charges can be joined together.

111.   **Answer (C) is correct.** The majority opinion in *Duncan* focuses almost exclusively on the historical reasons for the inclusion of a jury trial right in the United States Constitution:

> [T]he jury trial provisions . . . reflect a fundamental decision about the exercise of official power — a reluctance to entrust plenary powers over the life and liberty of the citizen to one judge or to a group of judges. Fear of unchecked power, so typical of our State and Federal Governments in other respects, found expression in the criminal law in this insistence upon community participation in the determination of guilt or innocence. *Duncan v. Louisiana*, 391 U.S. 145, 156 (1968).

Thus, finding that the right to a jury was among those "fundamental principles of liberty and justice which lie at the base of all our civil and political institutions," the *Duncan* Court ruled that it was applicable to the states through the Due Process Clause of the Fourteenth Amendment.

Answer (A) is incorrect. Accuracy in fact-finding was not the primary reason. *Duncan v. Louisiana* found a Sixth Amendment right to a jury trial in serious cases and specifically recognized that a bench trial is not necessarily unfair.

Answer (B) is incorrect. While jury participation may increase public respect for a verdict, the opinion of the court in *Duncan* did not focus on or discuss this as a rationale for recognizing the right to a jury trial. The Court did not rule that a jury would be more accurate in its ability to determine fact, but that it would be less susceptible to corruption or caprice.

Answer (D) is incorrect because the Court was not focused on educating the public, but rather whether the jury was fundamental to a defendant's right to a fair trial.

112.   The Sixth Amendment to the United States Constitution guarantees an adult criminal defendant charged with a serious offense the right to be tried by a jury. Whether an offense is "serious" in the constitutional sense is assessed by looking at the maximum *available* penalty for conviction of that offense. Any offense with a potential penalty of more than six months imprisonment is a serious offense, and any offense with a maximum penalty of six months or less is presumed to be petty and not implicate the right to a jury trial. *Duncan v. Louisiana*, 391 U.S. 145 (1968); *Baldwin v. New York*, 399 U.S. 66 (1970). Here, the maximum prison term is six months, one day under the sanction triggering the right to a jury trial under the Sixth Amendment.

However, an offense carrying a maximum sentence of six months or less may still be a serious offense if additional authorized penalties are so severe that they clearly reflect a legislative determination that the offense is a serious one. A fine of $10,000 in conjunction with a six-month term of imprisonment is not sufficiently serious as to entitle a defendant to a jury trial. *Blanton v. City of North Las Vegas*, 489 U.S. 538, 543 (1989). Here, the $700 fine is obviously insufficient to trigger the defendant's right to a jury trial.

The restitution obligation is irrelevant because for purposes of the right to a jury trial, restitution does not impose an additional obligation on the defendant; rather it recognizes the debt that the defendant already owes.

Under the U.S. Constitution, the defendant was not entitled to a jury trial.

113.   **Answer (C) is correct.** Under the Sixth Amendment to the United States Constitution, an offender is entitled to a jury trial in an "adult" court if the sentence carries more than six months' possible imprisonment. *Baldwin v. New York*, 399 U.S. 66 (1970). Here the standard is satisfied because the maximum sentence is nine months in prison. The defendant's age is irrelevant.

   Answers (A) and (D) are incorrect. A defendant in juvenile proceedings is not entitled to a jury trial under the Sixth Amendment, as such hearings are different in nature from normal criminal trials. A jury would tend to introduce an adversarial nature to the proceedings and hinder the cooperative, protective goals of juvenile proceedings. *McKeiver v. Pennsylvania*, 403 U.S. 528 (1971).

   Answer (B) is incorrect because the maximum sentence of exactly six months falls below the "more than" six-month "seriousness" threshold set by *Duncan v. Louisiana*, 391 U.S. 145 (1968) and *Baldwin v. New York*, 399 U.S. 66 (1970).

114.   Challenges for cause may be based on the lack of legal qualifications for service, a physical or mental inability to serve (such as pending surgery), important job or family responsibilities, or bias (sometimes even including implied bias). The fact that two potential jurors are married, alone, is unlikely to have them excluded for cause. There should be more exploration whether the two people will act independently of one another if both are on the same jury. But absent more information, they would have to be excluded through peremptory challenges rather than through a for-cause exclusion. *See generally Harris v. Commonwealth*, 313 S.W.3d 40 (Ky. 2010).

115.   **Answer (A) is correct** (*i.e.*, it is incorrect). This standard, articulated in *Witherspoon v. Illinois*, 391 U.S. 510 (1968), was rejected by the court in *Wainwright v. Witt*, discussed below.

   Answer (B) is incorrect (*i.e.*, it is a correct statement of the law). In *Wainwright v. Witt*, 469 U.S. 412 (1985), the Supreme Court announced this test as the proper one for "for-cause" challenges in the "death qualification" of potential capital jurors. Essentially, the Court held that a capital juror could be excluded for cause if unable to follow the law.

   Answer (C) is incorrect (*i.e.*, it is accurate). A juror who could not impose the death penalty because of his or her religious beliefs may be excluded for cause as being unable to follow the law. *See Wainwright v. Witt, supra*.

   Answer (D) is incorrect because answer (A) is an invalid test for excluding capital jurors for cause. Thus, all the answers are not accurate.

116.   In *Batson v. Kentucky*, 476 U.S. 79 (1986), the United States Supreme Court held that purposeful racial discrimination in jury selection violates the defendant's right to equal protection as well as the rights of the excluded group and those of the entire community. In *Davis v. Minnesota*, 511 U.S. 1115 (1994), the Court held that *Batson* also barred exercising

a peremptory challenge on the basis of a religious classification. *Davis*, however, did not bar all considerations of religion. A potential juror's religion may be a permissible ground for exclusion if the faith is relevant to an issue in the case.

In *Purkett v. Elem*, 514 U.S. 765 (1995), the Court may have made it easier for you to use your peremptory challenge to exclude jurors for religion-based reasons. *Purkett* held that the exercise of a peremptory challenge is permissible if counsel can establish a race-neutral explanation for the challenge. According to *Purkett*, this explanation does not have to be "persuasive, or even plausible."

In this case, it is unlikely that the juror's religion *per se* is relevant to an issue in the embezzlement case, but the juror's faith may be relevant if her religious affiliation would bias the potential juror against your client. If the potential juror knows the defendant or is offended by the theft from her church, the challenge may be permitted even though religion-based.

117. **Answer (D) is correct** (*i.e.*, it states an erroneous legal conclusion). The Constitution does not give the accused an absolute right to waive a jury. Rule 23(a) of the Federal Rules of Criminal Procedure provides that the government must consent to a waiver of jury trial. If the government does not consent, the court should empanel a jury, irrespective of the defendant's efforts to waive the jury.

Answer (A) is incorrect (*i.e.*, it is legally valid). Since the defendant has the right to have a jury trial, he or she must consent to any waiver of it. The waiver must be in writing. Rule 23(a). The three requirements for a valid waiver are that it must be knowing, intelligent, and voluntary. *See e.g., Schneckloth v. Bustamonte*, 412 U.S. 218 (1973).

Answer (B) is incorrect (*i.e.*, it is legally valid). Under Rule 23(a), a waiver of jury must be approved by the court, which must ensure that the waiver is knowing, intelligent, and voluntary.

Answer (C) is incorrect (*i.e.*, it is a legally valid). Under Rule 23(a), the government (as well as the judge and the defendant) must agree to a waiver of a jury trial.

118. **Answer (A) is correct.** A defendant's Sixth Amendment right to a jury trial does not guarantee a 12-member jury in state court. The Supreme Court approved the use of a jury in state cases with as few as six jurors in *Williams v. Florida*, 399 U.S. 78 (1970).

Answer (B) is incorrect according to *Williams v. Florida*, Deff had no constitutional right to a jury of 12. The harmless error issue is irrelevant since the jury was properly constituted.

Answer (C) is incorrect because juries smaller than 12 people were used even before the Bill of Rights was ratified. More importantly, the Supreme Court has not based the determination of jury size on historical figures, but rather on whether a specific jury size would adequately achieve the reasons for which the right to trial by jury was guaranteed. Some of those reasons are to prevent oppression by the government, to promote group deliberation, to insulate members from outside intimidation, and to provide a representative cross-section of the community. *Ballew v. Georgia*, 435 U.S. 223 (1978).

Answer (D) is incorrect as well. A jury of nine people is capable of achieving this purpose. *Williams v. Florida*, 399 U.S. 78 (1970).

119.   **Answer (B) is correct.** A defendant's right to a jury trial does not necessarily guarantee a 12-member jury. The Supreme Court has approved the use of a jury even as small as six persons. *Williams v. Florida*, 399 U.S. 78 (1970). However, a jury of five is too small to satisfy the Sixth Amendment.

Answer (A) is incorrect. The Supreme Court has also held, however, that a jury of five persons or smaller is not sufficiently large to achieve the reasons for which the right to trial by jury was guaranteed. Some of those reasons are to prevent government oppression by promoting group deliberation, insulating members from outside intimidation, and providing a representative cross-section of the community. *Ballew v. Georgia*, 435 U.S. 223 (1978).

Answers (C) and (D) are incorrect. Answer (D) is incorrect because juries with fewer than 12 people were used even before the Bill of Rights was ratified. More importantly, the Supreme Court has not based the determination of jury size on historical figures, but rather on whether a specific jury size would adequately achieve the reasons for which the right to trial by jury was guaranteed. Nor is the appropriate determination whether a larger jury would or would not have convicted the defendant; therefore Answer (C) is incorrect as well.

120.   Assuming your state's constitution does not mandate a unanimous jury verdict in criminal cases (as many state constitutions do), there is also no federal constitutional impediment to reducing the jury verdict requirement from unanimous to 10-2 in non-capital cases. In *Apodaca v. Oregon*, 406 U.S. 404 (1972), the United States Supreme Court upheld an Oregon law that permitted a criminal conviction by jury vote of 10-2. The less-than-unanimous rule, according to *Apodaca*, does not violate the cross-section requirement, since there is no guarantee that any particular jury would have members constituting a cross-section of the community, and it does not unconstitutionally impair the jury's functioning.

The wisdom of the non-unanimous verdict is another matter. It dilutes the impact of minority participants who no longer have a veto over the verdict. Moreover, it increases the likelihood that an innocent person will be convicted since the number of convictions will increase and the lone juror with doubts about guilt may well be ignored since his or her vote may be rendered irrelevant. On the other hand, it will result in fewer mistrials since 11-1 and 10-2 verdicts that formerly resulted in a hung jury will now result in a conviction or acquittal.

121.   **Answer (C) is correct.** As the Supreme Court has written:

> The purpose of the jury trial . . . is to prevent oppression by the Government. "Providing an accused with the right to be tried by a jury of his peers gave him an inestimable safeguard against the corrupt or overzealous prosecutor and against the compliant, biased, or eccentric judge." Given this purpose, the essential feature of a jury obviously lies in the interposition between the accused and his accuser of the commonsense judgment of a group of laymen, and in the community participation and shared responsibility that results from that group's determination of guilt or innocence.

Williams v. Florida, 399 U.S. 78, 100 (1970) (citation omitted). There was a systematic exclusion of a distinctive group. *See* below.

Answer (A) is incorrect. The Constitution is violated if there is a jury selection system in place that systematically under represents a distinctive group. "This prophylactic vehicle is not provided if the jury pool is made up of only special segments of the populace or if large, distinctive groups are excluded from the pool." *Taylor v. Louisiana*, 419 U.S. 522, 530 (1975). Therefore, "the selection of a petit jury from a representative cross section of the community is an essential component of the sixth amendment right to a jury trial. . . . the fair-cross-section requirement [is] fundamental to the jury trial guaranteed by the [s]ixth [a]mendment . . . ." *Id.* at 528, 530.

Answer (B) is incorrect. This ethnic group obviously meets the requirements that (1) it is a "distinctive" group; (2) the statistical disparity is not fair and reasonable; and (3) this under representation is due to a systematic exclusion of the group in the jury-selection process. *See Duren v. Missouri*, 439 U.S. 357 (1979). So, Daisy's Sixth Amendment right to a trial by jury was infringed, and she should have the right to be retried by a satisfactory jury, but not for the reason given in Answer (B). Whether the right is violated depends not on the final, actual composition of the *petit jury*, but on the systematic and unfair exclusion of a distinctive group from the jury selection process. *Taylor*, 419 U.S. at 530.

Answer (D) is incorrect. The right to a jury selected from a representative cross-section of the community is enforceable by the defendant, even though the exclusion might also involve a violation of the rights of members of the excluded segment of the community. Thus, the Supreme Court in *Taylor* allowed the defendant, a male, to challenge the exclusion of women from the Louisiana jury pool.

DEFENDANT'S RIGHT TO ATTEND TRIAL AND RELATED PROCEEDINGS

122. **Answer (B) is correct.** Rule 43 of the Federal Rules of Criminal Procedure (which codifies case law on some of the defendant's rights of confrontation and due process) states that the trial will proceed to completion and the defendant will be considered to have waived the right to be present whenever a defendant, initially present at trial, is voluntarily absent after the trial has commenced (whether or not the defendant has been informed by the court of the obligation to remain during the trial).

   Answer (A) is incorrect because in this scenario, the defendant was not present at the commencement of the trial, and therefore trial may not proceed in his absence. *Crosby v. U.S.*, 506 U.S. 255 (1993).

   Answer (C) is incorrect because the defendant's absence after trial begins may constitute a waiver of presence, but not if the defendant absconds before trial begins.

   Answer (D) is incorrect because defense counsel cannot waive a defendant's presence at the start of a felony trial. Under Rule 43, the accused must be present personally at that time.

123. **Answer (D) is correct.** The defendant's Sixth Amendment and due process rights to attend trial do not include argument in the appellate court. These rights are restricted to trial-related proceedings and do not reach proceedings only involving questions of law. There would also be serious security concerns if the accused had to be transported long distances to appellate courts lacking adequate secure lock-up facilities.

   Answers (A), (B), and (C) are incorrect because the defendant's right to attend trial includes jury selection, the entire trial, and announcement of the verdict.

124. You should deny the motion for a mistrial and complete the proceeding. A criminal accused has a Sixth Amendment (confrontation) and due process right to attend his or her trial. However, a trial judge has the discretion to remove a disruptive defendant from the courtroom and proceed with the trial. *Illinois v. Allen*, 397 U.S. 337, 343–44 (1970).

   The leading case, *Illinois v. Allen*, 397 U.S. 337, 343–44 (1970), gives the judge considerable latitude in dealing with the disruptive defendant. As noted in the next question, the judge may bind and gag the accused, cite the accused for contempt, or remove the accused from the courtroom until the accused promises to act appropriately. Since Mann was highly disruptive the judge clearly warned him and told him he could return if he acted in an appropriate manner, the judge should deny Mann's motion for a mistrial. The judge acted properly in dealing with a difficult situation.

125. **Answer (D) is correct.** An instruction allowing the jury to use the defendant's trial conduct in assessing guilt is not one of the options approved in *Illinois v. Allen*, 397 U.S. 337 (1970).

   Answers (A), (B), and (C) are incorrect. Each represents one of the three options that

Illinois v. Allen held was permissible in some situations in dealing with a disruptive criminal defendant.

126. The Sixth Amendment guarantees a defendant that "[i]n all criminal prosecutions, the accused shall enjoy the right to a . . . public trial." This establishes a strong presumption in favor of openness and free access to criminal trials. Therefore, any party seeking to close the courtroom "must advance an overriding interest that is likely to be prejudiced, the closure must be no broader than necessary to protect that interest, the trial court must consider reasonable alternatives to closing the proceeding, and it must make findings adequate to support the closure." *Waller v. Georgia*, 467 U.S. 39, 48 (1984). The courtroom in *Waller* was closed to prevent the public and press from hearing audiotapes of wiretaps, because the state feared that persons other than the defendant would have their privacy invaded.

Here, however, the courtroom was not actually closed. There was no motion or order to prevent the public and press from attending. There was no attempt to restrict the flow of information to the press or shield the proceedings from public scrutiny. The public, as a whole, was present. Surely limiting the number of observers is reasonable considering the size of the courtroom and the possible fire hazard involved. Since the courtroom was never actually closed, Daniel's right to a public trial was not violated. [Based on *Wilson v. State*, 814 A.2d 1 (Md. App. 2002).]

127. **Answer (A) is correct** (*i.e.*, it is not a legitimate reason). Closing court proceedings to the public whenever a minor sexual assault victim testifies is not permissible. However, closure for this reason is permissible on a case-by-case basis when necessary to protect the psychological and physical welfare of this particular victim.

Answer (B) is incorrect (*i.e.*, it is a legitimate reason). Judges may also close or limit access to the courts in order to protect a witness, defendant, or victim from threats that may have been made. Similarly, it may be necessary in some instances to protect a particular crime victim from public exposure when the nature of the crime, the victim's age, and the psychological condition of the victim are highly sensitive. *Globe Newspaper Co. v. Superior Court*, 457 U.S. 596, 608 (1982).

Answer (C) is incorrect (*i.e.*, it is a legitimate reason). Court proceedings may be closed when national security dictates keeping certain matters confidential and when opening the proceedings would violate that need. *Richmond Newspapers, Inc. v. Virginia*, 448 U.S. 555, 598 n.24 (1980).

Answer (D) is incorrect (*i.e.*, it is a legitimate reason). Court proceedings may be closed for a portion of a trial in order to protect the life and identity of an undercover agent, but there must be a specific finding that in the particular case the closure is necessary.

128. **Answer (A) is correct.** "[T]he First Amendment guarantees of speech and press, standing alone, prohibit government from summarily closing courtroom doors which had long been open to the public at the time that Amendment was adopted. . . . [T]he right [of the public] to attend criminal trials is implicit in the guarantees of the First Amendment. . . . Absent an overriding interest articulated in findings, the trial of a criminal case must be open to the public." *Richmond Newspapers, Inc. v. Virginia*, 448 U.S. 555, 576, 580–581 (1980). Here, the judge's blanket order violates the First Amendment, and Answer (A) is a valid argument. Therefore, **Answer (D) is incorrect.**

Answers (B) and (C) are incorrect. The newspaper cannot, however, argue the Sixth Amendment in support of its injunction. The right to a public trial under the Sixth Amendment is a right personally possessed by the defendant alone (who may have waived it anyway). *Gannett Co., Inc. v. DePasquale*, 443 U.S. 368, 379–380 (1979).

Answer (D) is incorrect for the reason stated above.

129. **Answer (C) is correct.** Many cases refuse to overturn a trial because of a Sixth Amendment violation unless the accused made a timely objection to the closure. The issue is considered waived since the trial court did not have an opportunity to rectify the situation.

Answer (A) is incorrect. For a substantial violation of the Sixth Amendment's public trial guarantee, no showing of prejudice is needed or, indeed, could actually be proven. *Arizona v. Fulminante*, 499 U.S. 279 (1991).

Answer (B) is incorrect. A denial of a public trial is not subject to harmless error review. *Arizona v. Fulminante*, 499 U.S. 279 (1991) (denial of public trial is structural defect; harmless error analysis not used).

Answer (D) is incorrect. The fact that some members of the public were permitted to attend will not doom an appeal since the Sixth Amendment requires that trials generally be open to the public unless there is a specific reason for a total or partial closure. Here, there was no justification since there were no findings that the child-witnesses could not testify fully if the courtroom were open to the general public.

130. Yes, the criminal defendant does have a right to testify at the defendant's own trial, although the Constitution contains no specific language recognizing this right. Nevertheless, in *Rock v. Arkansas*, 483 U.S. 44 (1987), the United States Supreme Court recognized that the right to testify and be heard in one's own defense is one the fundamental rights protected by Due Process Clauses of the Fifth and Fourteenth Amendments, and by the Compulsory Process Clause of the Sixth Amendment.

The Court in *Rock* reasoned that the Compulsory Process Clause gives the accused the right to call helpful witnesses, including even the accused, who may be the most important defense witness to testify. A related source cited by *Rock* is the Sixth Amendment's guarantee of the right of the accused personally to make his or her defense, which includes the right personally to call favorable witnesses, including the defendant himself or herself. Still another source is the Fifth Amendment's guarantee against self-incrimination. The *Rock* Court expansively read this right as guaranteeing both the right to remain silent and the right to testify.

It is clear Darwin was not accorded this important right and it is likely the conviction will be reversed.

131. **Answer (A) is correct.** Every criminal defendant has the right to remain silent and not testify at his or her criminal trial. The right is guaranteed by the Fifth Amendment and is applied to the states by the Fourteenth Amendment. Allowing the prosecutor to comment at all on the defendant's choice to remain silent would allow the prosecutor to penalize the defendant for exercising the constitutional right. The clear intent would be to induce the defendant not to take the stand. Such an effect would be even more severe if the court instructed the jury that the defendant's choice reflected on the evidence. *Griffin v. California*, 380 U.S. 609 (1965).

Answer (B) is incorrect. The judge may instruct the jury not to consider the defendant's choice to exercise the defendant's Fifth Amendment rights. A different conclusion would require the assumptions that (1) the jurors did not notice the fact that the defendant kept silent, and (2) they will ignore the judge's instructions and hold against the defendant the very thing they were told to disregard. "Federal constitutional law cannot rest on speculative assumptions so dubious as these." *Lakeside v. Oregon*, 435 U.S. 333, 340 (1978).

Answer (C) is incorrect because the prosecutor may comment on the defendant's opportunity to conform the defendant's testimony to that of other witnesses. According to the Supreme Court, such an argument would be a comment upon the defendant's credibility as a witness, not a suggestion that the exercise of the defendant's right not to testify is evidence of guilt. *Portuondo v. Agard*, 529 U.S. 61 (2000).

Answer (D) is incorrect. The prosecutor's statements about Quiet would be unconstitutional. Since Answer (A) reflects an unconstitutional statement by the prosecution, **Answer (D) is incorrect.**

132.   **Answer (B) is correct.** The Due Process Clause of both the Fifth and Fourteenth Amendment guarantees that a defendant may only be convicted "upon proof beyond a reasonable doubt of every fact necessary to constitute the crime with which [the defendant] has been charged." *In re Winship*, 397 U.S. 358, 364 (1970). By creating a presumption about the defendant's intent that the jury is required to apply, the instruction would relieve the state of the burden of proving the element of intent. *Francis v. Franklin*, 471 U.S. 307 (1985). Therefore, Proposed Jury Instruction #2 is unconstitutional.

   Answer (A) is incorrect because it is constitutionally permissible to require the defendant to prove "affirmative" defenses such as self-defense. Instruction #1 is constitutional. Thus, Answer (D) is incorrect, as well.

   Answer (C) is incorrect. It is a constitutional jury instruction because it does not require the jury to apply a presumption about the defendant's intent. The instruction affirms a "permissive inference," clarifying that the jury may find intent based upon circumstantial evidence, just as it may do with any other element. It does not shift the burden of proof.

   Answer (D) is incorrect because Answers (A) and (C) are constitutional; only answer (B) is unconstitutional.

133.   **Answer (C) is the best answer.** While the United States Supreme Court has held that the state has the burden of persuasion on each element of the crime, it has not provided specific guidance on the burdens for defenses. In *Patterson v. New York*, 432 U.S. 197 (1977), the Supreme Court indicated that states are free to allocate the burden of persuasion and the standard of proof for traditional defenses as they see fit. Accordingly, since Answers (A) and (B) are correct and states are free to adopt either of them, Answer (C), embracing (A) and (B), is the best answer.

   Answer (D) is incorrect since both Answers (A) and (B) are permissible options for states to choose in allocating the standard of proof and burden of persuasion for an insanity defense.

134.   **Answer (B) is correct.** In the federal system and that of many states, the prosecutor actually makes two closing arguments. Federal Rule of Criminal Procedure 29.1 states clearly that the prosecution gives the first closing argument, then defense counsel gives her closing, then the prosecutor is given a chance to rebut the defense's closing argument.

Answers (A) and (C) are not correct. Under Rule 29.1 the prosecutor does address the jury before the defense closing and then possibly again after the defense closing.

Answer (D) is incorrect because it is unlikely that a court would permit a prosecutor to make a jury argument when the jury returns to the courtroom to have a question resolved. Closing arguments are made before the jury retires to deliberate.

135. Rule 30 of the Federal Rules of Criminal Procedure prescribes the steps necessary to present a proposed jury instruction. First, counsel must file a written request that the judge give the proposed instructions. Though the rule does not so specify, the request should indicate the exact language counsel wants the judge to use.

Second, the request must be timely. Rule 30(a) provides that the request must be made at the close of evidence, unless Judge Huang has established an earlier, reasonable time.

Finally, the requesting party must provide every other party with a copy of the written request.

136. **Answer (C) is correct.** Rule 30(b) requires Judge Huang to rule on the request and so inform the parties before their closing arguments. This will enable the parties to use the ruling in fashioning their closing arguments.

Answer (A) is incorrect since Rule 30 does not adopt the "as soon as possible" standard though surely counsel would appreciate an early decision.

Answer (B) is incorrect because jury instructions are not finalized until after the evidence is presented by both sides. Developments during the defense case may have to be dealt with in the jury instructions.

Answer (D) is incorrect since Rule 30(b) requires a ruling before closing statements so the parties may use the actual jury instructions in their closings.

137. Rule 30(d) states that a party objecting to any portion of the jury instructions or, as in this case, a failure to give a jury instruction must inform the court of the specific objection and the grounds for the objection. In order to give the judge an opportunity to correct any error, the objection must be made before the jury retires to deliberate.

To protect the jury from being confused and to avoid any possible prejudice to the parties, Rule 30 further says that Judge Huang must give defense counsel an opportunity to make this objection out of the jury's hearing and, upon defense counsel's request, the jury's presence. A failure to follow this procedure will ordinarily bar appellate review of the jury instruction issue, unless the court permits it to be considered under Rule 52(b) as plain error.

138.   **Answer (B) is correct.** A special verdict, as opposed to a general verdict, requires the jury to answer specific fact questions, usually addressing whether the facts prove a specific element of the crime. For example, in a burglary, a special verdict may mandate that the jury decide whether the illegal entry was made "with the intent to commit a crime inside the building."

Answer (A) is incorrect. Though special verdicts are used to some extent in capital sentencing cases when the jury must made a finding whether specific aggravating or mitigating circumstances are present, the special verdict may also be used in non-capital cases.

Answer (C) is incorrect. In general, whether a special verdict is used does not depend on whether it was requested by the defendant or prosecution, or selected by the court acting on its own. Some jurisdictions however, disallow special verdicts if the defendant objects to their use.

Answer (D) is incorrect. Though some defendants have argued that the special verdict violates due process because it makes it more difficult for jury nullification, the use of the special verdict does not violate due process. *See e.g., Black v. U.S.*, 561 U.S. 465 (2010) (suggesting that special verdict in complex cases "can be extremely useful").

139.   **Answer (D) is correct.** In most American jurisdictions, inconsistent verdicts are upheld. *See e.g., U.S. v. Powell*, 469 U.S. 57 (1984) (inconsistent verdicts should not be reviewable).

Answers (A), (B), and (C), are incorrect. Inconsistent verdicts are generally valid because their meaning is unclear. They may reflect sympathy for the accused or antipathy toward the accused; their meaning is speculative. The accused may always appeal any conviction but an appeal solely because of the inconsistency will likely not succeed.

140. **Answer (C) is correct.** Though juries seem to have the power of jury nullification, most jurisdictions do not permit jury instructions authorizing jury nullification.

Answer (A) is incorrect. A potential juror may be excused from jury service if he or she claims the power not to follow the law in resolving the case.

Answer (B) is incorrect. Courts generally do not require jury instructions on jury nullification. Hence, most juries are not instructed that they actually do have the power of nullification.

Answer (D) is incorrect. Many jurisdictions do not permit counsel to argue for jury nullification. The general position is that juries are to follow the law, not act irrespective of the law. This engenders the unusual result that juries usually do have the power of nullification but do not know that they do.

141. An *"Allen* charge" (sometimes referred to as a "dynamite charge"), named after the Supreme Court's decision in *Allen v. U.S.*, 164 U.S. 492 (1896), is a jury instruction given to a deadlocked jury. Designed to encourage the jurors to reach a decision, it instructs the jurors that it is their duty to decide the case and it tells jurors to listen to the opinions of others and give those opinions appropriate deference. More particularly, it urges jurors holding a minority position to reassess the perceived correctness of their views.

142. **Answer (A) is correct.** The primary criticism is that it coerces the minority into agreeing with the majority, thus, in practice, increasing guilty verdicts, decreasing hung juries, and depriving people with minority views of the full measure of their independence.

Answer (B) is incorrect because the real brunt of *Allen* is to coerce the minority jurors, not the majority ones.

Answer (C) is incorrect because an *Allen* charge produces more convictions than acquittals. The minority jurors asked to reconsider their votes are routinely holdouts for acquittal rather than conviction.

Answer (D) is incorrect since the *Allen* charged is designed to reduce the number of hung juries, not increase their number.

143. The Sixth Amendment to the United States Constitution provides that "[i]n all criminal prosecutions, the accused shall enjoy the right to a speedy . . . trial . . . ." In *Barker v. Wingo*, 407 U.S. 514 (1972), the Supreme Court refused to set specific parameters on this right and adopted a flexible, factor-based approach to resolving the issue of when the accused's speedy trial rights have been violated.

The first factor is the length of the delay between the initiation of criminal proceedings (the arrest or indictment) and the criminal trial. The length of this delay is considered to be a "triggering mechanism" and is "presumptively prejudicial" as it approaches a year. *Doggett v. U.S.*, 505 U.S. 647 (1992). Here, Kidd was tried and convicted (August 1st a year ago) more than 45 months after he was indicted (February 1st, four years ago), a length of time triggering a possible Sixth Amendment claim.

The second *Barker* factor is the reason for the delay. In the instant case, the first trial was scheduled in October, three years ago and was postponed a total of eight times. The first (October 1st, three years ago) and two other postponements were because of defense needs (defendant's new lawyer needed time to prepare; new defense alibi witness possible, and defendant's lawyer had a trial conflict). Three others were for administrative reasons unrelated to either party (bomb scare, ill judge, unavailable courtroom), and two were attributed to the prosecution (child birth, missing witness). Since two of the delays were to assist the government in presenting its best case, it may be that this factor will be so decisive that it will cause a Sixth Amendment violation, though this conclusion is far from certain. Delays by defense counsel are attributed to the defendant. *Vermont v. Brillon*, 556 U.S. 81 (2009).

The third *Barker* factor is whether the accused demanded a speedy trial. The defendant specifically objected to two postponements (February 15th, two years ago, and the one for the head prosecutor's child birth — you argued the assistant prosecutor was prepared to handle the case for the government). Thus, the defendant did demand a speedy trial and this factor may have been satisfied, though the defendant requested a continuance three times (new lawyer, new possible alibi witness, and trial conflict).

The fourth *Barker* factor is prejudice to the accused. Defendant Kidd must establish that the delay somehow prejudiced his ability adequately to present the case at trial. Based on the facts in the question, there is no obvious prejudice. The government's case was very strong and Kidd's quite weak. The alibi witness, who was not sure that he saw Kidd in the woods at the time of the kidnapping, died before trial but would have been available had the trial occurred earlier. This person was a very poor defense witness, especially when compared to the strong eyewitness testimony, the unanimous identification at the lineup, Kidd's green van with the license tag that matched, in part, the one seen by the eyewitness, and Kidd's escape to Mexico.

144. **Answer (C) is correct.** In *Smith v. Hooey*, 393 U.S. 374 (1969), the United States Supreme

Court held that the Sixth Amendment speedy trial guarantee protects prisoners incarcerated in a state other than one that has issued an indictment against the prisoner. Upon that prisoner's demand, the jurisdiction that issued the indictment must make a "diligent, good faith effort" to bring the prisoner before its courts for trial. American jurisdictions have signed the Interstate Compact on Detainers that facilitates this interstate cooperation.

Answers (A) and (B) are incorrect because *Smith v. Hooey* held that the speedy trial guarantee does apply to persons charged with crimes who are incarcerated in another jurisdiction.

Answer (D) is incorrect because *Smith* does not mandate a trial in the State of Boerum (where he is incarcerated) of the homicide charges pending in the State of Brooke. Trial will be in Brooke.

145.   **Answer (B) is correct.** Under 18 U.S.C. § 3161(b), ordinarily an indictment must be filed within 30 days of arrest if the federal grand jury is in session. If the federal grand jury is not in session, an additional 30 days is permitted.

      Answers (A), (C), and (D) are incorrect because they state inaccurate time periods in which an indictment must be filed.

146.   **Answer (B) is correct.** Under 18 U.S.C. § 3161(c) ordinarily trial should commence within 70 days from the filing of the indictment or information. If the accused is indicted and then taken before a judicial officer, the date the accused appears before the judicial officer begins the 70-day time limit.

      Answers (A), (C), and (D) are incorrect because each states an inaccurate time period.

147.   **Answer (C) is the correct answer.** Under the federal Speedy Trial Act, 18 U.S.C. § 3161(c), ordinarily trial should commence within 70 days from the filing of the indictment or information. The constitutional speedy trial guarantee has no specific limit and, using the factor approach in *Barker v. Wingo*, 407 U.S. 514 (1972), the time limit would be far longer than 70 days. There is a one-year "trigger" that sets the time when the speedy trial constitutional guarantee begins to establish a meaningful deadline. *Doggett v. U.S.*, 505 U.S. 647 (1992).

      Answers (A) and (B) are incorrect because the time limit for the speedy trial statute is far shorter than that for the constitutional provision.

      Answer (D) is incorrect because the constitutional speedy trial guarantee does apply to the time between indictment and trial.

148.   **Answer (D) is correct** because the time it took the government to relocate missing evidence is not an exception under 18 U.S.C. § 3161(h).

      Answers (A), (B), and (C) are incorrect (because they are exceptions). The time it took the government to respond to any pretrial motion is excluded under 18 U.S.C. § 3161(h)(1)(D) (Answer (A)); the time to resolve the interlocutory appeal is excluded under 18 U.S.C. § 3161(h)(1)(C) (Answer (B)); and the time to conduct a mental examination of Mary Linda is also excluded under 18 U.S.C. § 3161(h)(1)(A) (Answer (C)).

149.   Two limits exist with respect to setting criminal cases too quickly. First, the defendant has a

due process right to a fair opportunity to prepare a defense. This may also be part of the accused's Sixth Amendment right to the effective assistance of counsel. Scheduling a case too promptly may well violate this important right.

Second, the Federal Speedy Trial Act of 1974, 18 U.S.C. § 3161(c)(2), provides that absent the defendant's consent in writing, a trial shall not commence less than 30 days from the date the defendant first appears through counsel.

150. **Answer (A) is correct.** The statute of limitations begins to run from the time of the crime and ordinarily ends at arrest or indictment. Sometimes the starting date is difficult to establish if the precise date of the offense is uncertain.

Answers (B), (C), and (D) are incorrect because these dates do not determine when the statute of limitation begins to run. Some of these dates may be important in assessing when the statute of limitations *stops* running. Typically, the statute of limitations ceases to run when the defendant is arrested or indicted.

151. **Answer (A) is correct.** The statute of limitations runs from the time of the crime to the time of formal charges, such as an indictment.

Answers (B), (C), and (D) are incorrect because the statute of limitations ordinarily would have stopped running at the indictment (Answer (A)).

152. **Answer (C) is correct.** When a statute of limitations is tolled, it stops running temporarily. The period during which it is tolled does not count in assessing whether the statute was violated. For example, by statute often the statute of limitations is tolled during the time the defendant is out of state. Thus, if the defendant commits a crime on January 1st and immediately leaves the state to avoid apprehension, the statute of limitations does not run during the defendant's absence from the state.

Answer (A) is incorrect because tolling deals with an interruption in the running of the statute of limitations, not in the fact that it was exceeded.

Answer (B) is incorrect since tolling means the running of the statute is interrupted, not that it has started to run.

Answer (D) is incorrect since tolling means that the running of the statute is interrupted. By definition, the initial event starting the statute has occurred.

153. **Answer (B) is correct.** The Fifth Amendment states that "No person shall . . . be subject for the same offense to be twice put in jeopardy of life or limb. . . . " Despite its broad language, the provision makes clear that the concept of "same offense" is pivotal to any interpretation. Similarly, it must be decided what constitutes being in "jeopardy."

Answer (A) is incorrect because the Fifth Amendment does not specifically mention "conviction."

Answer (C) is similarly incorrect because the phrase "double jeopardy" does not appear in the Amendment despite the common reference to the Double Jeopardy Clause of the Fifth Amendment.

Answer (D) is incorrect because the word "trial" is not in the amendment. Plus, this provision as interpreted by the Supreme Court, does not bar all second trials for the same crime. For example, a second trial after some mistrials is permissible under the Double Jeopardy Clause.

154. **Answer (C) is correct.** Double jeopardy does not bar a second trial for a mistrial following a hung jury. In *U.S. v. Perez*, 22 U.S. 579 (1824), the Supreme Court held that a mistrial caused by a hopelessly deadlocked jury does not bar a retrial since there has been no final verdict and society has an important interest in giving the prosecution one complete opportunity to convict persons believed to have violated laws. *See also Arizona v. Washington*, 434 U.S. 497 (1978).

Answers (A), (B), and (D) are incorrect because they represent the three categories of results traditionally barred by the double jeopardy guarantee. *See North Carolina v. Pearce*, 395 U.S. 711, 717 (1969).

155. **Answer (C) is correct** because neither Answer (A) nor (B) would permit a retrial over a double jeopardy objection. A jury acquittal bars the second prosecution. *U.S. v. Ball*, 163 U.S. 662 (1896). This has been justified as countering "an unacceptably high risk that the Government, with its vastly superior resources, might wear down the defendant so that 'even though innocent, he may be found guilty.' " *U.S. v. Scott*, 437 U.S. 82 (1978).

Answers (A) and (B) are correct but not the best answer. Even though a jury acquittal was based on jury error or malfeasance, the acquittal is effective to bar future prosecutions for the same offense.

Answer (D) is incorrect since both answers (A) and (B) would bar a retrial following an acquittal even if the acquittal is based on misunderstanding the jury instructions or bribed jurors.

156. **Answer (D) is correct.** Once a judge grants an acquittal on the basis of insufficient evidence, it is a final decision even if granted by mistake.

Answers (A) and (B) are incorrect. An acquittal by the judge still bars retrial even if the acquittal is based on a misunderstanding of the applicable law or the erroneous exclusion of key government evidence that essentially gutted the prosecution's case. *See Sanabria v. U.S.*, 437 U.S. 54 (1978).

Answer (C) is incorrect. Once a judge issues an acquittal, he or she may not have a change of mind and retract the acquittal.

157. The defense motion is likely to be granted and a new trial barred. Under the Double Jeopardy Clause, when the defense objects to a mistrial, a retrial is still permitted if there was "manifest necessity" for the mistrial or if the ends of justice would be defeated by a retrial. *U.S. v. Dinitz*, 424 U.S. 600 (1976).

In a case such as this where the defendant did not request a mistrial, and indeed where neither the prosecutor nor defense lawyer had a chance to do so, the key question is whether there were effective alternatives to the mistrial. Here, the judge did not appear to explore any alternatives to declaring a mistrial. He was so angry he just dismissed the jury and left the courtroom. Though Judge O'Reilly was understandably enraged by Washington's insulting comments, there was still no legal reason to declare a mistrial. There were alternatives, such as taking a break to allow everyone to regain composure or to conduct a hearing (outside the jury's presence) to consider whether Washington should be held in contempt and to warn him about future outbursts. This may suggest that there was no manifest necessity for a mistrial and, therefore, retrial is barred. *See U.S. v. Jorn*, 400 U.S. 470 (1971) (judge declared a mistrial to allow prosecution witnesses to seek counsel to guard against self-incrimination; no alternatives to mistrial considered; double jeopardy barred retrial after the mistrial).

Another consideration is whether the prosecution acted in bad faith in causing the mistrial. Here, there is no evidence of prosecutorial bad faith or even involvement in the need for a mistrial.

158. The prosecution's motion will likely be granted and a new trial date set. The defense's motion to bar future proceedings because of double jeopardy concerns will be denied. When the defense requests the mistrial, re-prosecution is usually allowed under the Double Jeopardy Clause. In *U.S. v. Dinitz*, 424 U.S. 600 (1976), the Supreme Court held that when the defendant asks for the mistrial, he or she has essentially made a decision whether to continue with the trial, despite the errors, or to surrender the right to have the matter resolved by the original jury.

The primary exception is when the defendant is provoked into requesting a mistrial because of the intentional misbehavior by the prosecution. Perhaps the prosecutor is motivated by a desire to gain an advantage by starting anew or by a desire to harass the accused by forcing a second trial. *Oregon v. Kennedy*, 456 U.S. 667 (1982). In the instant case, there is no hint that the prosecution intentionally provoked the defense into requesting the mistrial.

159. **Answer (B) is correct.** Under *Blockburger v. U.S.*, 284 U.S. 299 (1932), the Supreme Court announced the test for determining whether two crimes are the "same offense" for purposes of double jeopardy analysis. The *Blockburger* test, often referred to as the same element or same evidence test, is whether "each provision requires proof of a fact which the other does not." This means that if transportation of a firearm across state lines is proved every time an alien in possession of a firearm is proved, the two crimes are the "same offense."

Answer (A) is incorrect. Answer (A) is not the best answer because *some* common elements are ordinarily insufficient to satisfy *Blockburger*.

Answer (C) is incorrect because the legislature's intent is not part of the test for determining whether double jeopardy would be offended by a second *trial* for the same offense.

Answer (D) is incorrect. Whether or not the two crimes occurred during the same transaction or time period is irrelevant under *Blockburger*, which focuses on elements and proof rather than time periods.

160. In *Ashe v. Swenson*, 397 U.S. 436 (1970), the United States Supreme Court held that collateral estoppel applied to criminal cases pursuant to the double jeopardy guarantee. The prosecution may not re-litigate issues already resolved in the defendant's favor in a prior prosecution. In the facts of the question, it is possible, though unlikely, that collateral estoppel will bar the second trial. The record of the first case will have to be reviewed carefully to ascertain exactly what issue the first jury resolved when it acquitted the defendant.

If the proof showed that only one person committed both assaults and the jury acquitted the defendant because he was not the person who committed the first assault, collateral estoppel could bar the second prosecution. On the other hand, if the acquittal in the first case was not based on identity or if different people could have committed the two assaults, collateral estoppel would not bar the second trial. Even if Jamison was not the person who assaulted the victim at the earlier time, he may have been the perpetrator of the second assault. Also, if the jury found that an element of the charged offense was not proven in the first trial, that element may have been present during the second offense.

161. **Answer (C) is correct.** This case involves the reach of double jeopardy *in a single trial*. Unlike the situation where there are multiple trials, in the case of a single trial the double jeopardy test is not *Blockburger*; it is one of statutory construction. A court asks whether the legislature intended for there to be cumulative punishment for the two applicable criminal statutes. *See Missouri v. Hunter*, 459 U.S. 359 (1983).

Answer (A) is incorrect because the double jeopardy test has nothing to do with the timing of the two events.

Answer (B) is incorrect because similarity of elements, such as possession, is not a dispositive issue when crimes are joined in a single trial. The key is what the legislature intended.

Answer (D) is incorrect because the *Blockburger* test does not apply to multiple punishments in the same trial; it applies only to sequential proceedings. Note that here it is likely that *Blockburger*, if it were the test, would not bar convictions or sentences since there are clearly distinct elements for the two crimes.

162. **Answer (D) is correct.** In *North Carolina v. Pearce*, 395 U.S. 711 (1969), the United States Supreme Court held that due process prohibits a state from imposing a harsher sentence on retrial for the purpose of punishing the defendant who successfully appeals a conviction. But an increased sentence is permissible, according to *Pearce*, if the record reflects objective information that the defendant's conduct since the new trial merited the increased sanction.

This will overcome the presumption of vindictiveness triggered by the harsher penalty.

Here, the defendant's new arson conviction could merit an increased punishment after the retrial, even though the conduct underlying it (the second arson) actually occurred before the first arson conviction. Because the second arson conviction occurred *after* the first one, it could be considered under *Pearce* in assessing punishment for the first conviction following a retrial of the first crime. *See Texas v. McCullough*, 475 U.S. 134 (1986).

Answer (A) is incorrect because *Pearce* clearly held that double jeopardy does not bar an increased sentence after retrial in some circumstances.

Answer (B) is incorrect because *Pearce* also held that equal protection was not violated since the defendant could receive exactly the same sentence after each trial.

Answer (C) is incorrect because *Pearce* places some limits on the sentence after a retrial.

163.   **Answer (C) is correct.** In a jury trial, the double jeopardy guarantee attaches once the entire jury is selected (empaneled) and sworn in. It does not apply to any prior proceedings. *Crist v. Bretz*, 437 U.S. 28 (1978). Here, the jury was selected but not sworn when the judge died.

Answers (A) and (B) are incorrect because double jeopardy does not attach at early trial stages such as the beginning of jury selection or when an indictment is issued.

Answer (D) is incorrect because in a jury trial jeopardy has already attached before the first witness takes the stand. *See Crist v. Bretz*, 437 U.S. 28 (1978). The jury would already have been selected and sworn.

164.   **Answer (D) is correct.** In non-jury cases, jeopardy attaches when the first witness for the prosecution is sworn. *See Crist v. Bretz*, 437 U.S. 28 (1978).

Answers (A), (B), and (C) are incorrect because they are all at later stages, after the first witness is sworn in a bench trial.

165.   **Answer (D) is correct.** Double jeopardy bars a retrial if the appellate court reversed because the government's evidence at trial was insufficient. *See Burks v. U.S.*, 437 U.S. 1 (1978). The government had a fair opportunity to present its best case and the Double Jeopardy Clause bars giving the government a second opportunity to obtain a conviction.

Answer (B) is incorrect. By way of contrast (and not necessarily clear logic), if the reversal was based on dissatisfaction with the *weight* of evidence rather than the *sufficiency* of the evidence, retrial is permissible. *See Tibbs v. Florida*, 457 U.S. 31 (1982).

Answers (A) and (C) are incorrect. When the appellate reversal is because of a trial error, retrial is ordinarily permitted. The defendant has chosen to take an appeal and has a legitimate interest in a readjudication free from judicial error. Answers (A) and (C) are incorrect because these "trial error" grounds do not bar retrial. If the Supreme Court cannot tell whether the reversal was for trial error or insufficient evidence, it may remand for clarification. *Greene v. Massey*, 437 U.S. 19 (1978).

166.   This question raises the so-called "separate sovereign doctrine" that allows more than one jurisdiction to prosecute a person for the identical conduct.

Answer (D) is correct because state and local governments are considered the same sovereign for double jeopardy purposes. Thus, Chicago, located in the State of Illinois, may not pursue charges for the same crimes prosecuted by Illinois. The two are not considered separate sovereigns under the Double Jeopardy Clause.

Answers (A), (B), and (C) are incorrect. Under the "separate sovereign" or "dual sovereign" doctrine, double jeopardy does not bar prosecution by different government entities. The underlying theory is that a crime is an offense against the sovereignty of each governmental unit having jurisdiction over a criminal act. *See Heath v. Alabama*, 474 U.S. 82 (1985). The federal government and each state are considered separate sovereigns and may each prosecute crimes over which they have jurisdiction. Thus, Illinois and Wisconsin (Answer (B)); the United States and Illinois (Answer (A)); and the United States and Chicago (Answer (C)) are all considered separate sovereigns and may each pursue a prosecution of Heade.

167. **Answer (D) is correct.** Although there was no majority opinion that explained the holding in *Furman*, the case has come to stand for the proposition that the death penalty cannot be imposed in ways that are arbitrary and capricious. That is, there must be some rational explanation for who lives and who dies. *Gregg v. Georgia*, 428 U.S. 153 (1976).

   Answers (A), (B), and (C), are incorrect since *Furman* was based on the greater issue of imposing death under the Eighth Amendment. While issues of race, international law, and method of execution are significant issues in the death penalty, these were not the prime focus of the *Furman* Court's analysis or opinions.

168. **Answer (D) is correct.** Individuals convicted of felony murder are eligible for the death penalty. *Tison v. Arizona*, 481 U.S. 137 (1987). However, this class of eligible offenders is limited to those who are a major participant in the felony and display a reckless indifference to human life in the commission of the felony.

   Answer (A) is incorrect because the Supreme Court categorically barred the execution of individuals who commit capital murder before the age of 18. *Roper v. Simmons*, 543 U.S. 551 (2005).

   Answer (B) is incorrect. The Supreme Court barred the execution of individuals with significantly sub-average intellectual capacity. *Atkins v. Virginia*, 536 U.S. 304 (2002).

   Answer (C) is incorrect. In *Ford v. Wainwright*, 477 U.S. 399 (1986), the Court held that the Eighth Amendment prohibited the execution of a mentally incompetent person. This does not prevent the execution of a person with severe mental illness who is diagnosed as "insane" unless the insanity also renders the person incompetent to truly understand the execution and the reasons for it. *Panetti v. Quarterman*, 551 U.S. 930 (2007).

169. **Answer (D) is correct.** The Supreme Court has limited the types of criminal activity for which the death penalty may be imposed. It has specifically approved that penalty for a defendant who does not actually kill but had major participation in a felony resulting in a death combined with reckless indifference to human life. *Tison v. Arizona*, 481 U.S. 137 (1987).

   Answers (A) and (B) are incorrect. The Court has specifically rejected the death penalty for rape of an adult (*Coker v. Georgia*, 433 U.S. 584 (1977)) or child (*Kennedy v. Louisiana*, 554 U.S. 407 (2008)).

   Answer (C) is incorrect. In *Enmund v. Florida*, 458 U.S. 782 (1982), the Court invalidated the death penalty for an accomplice to criminal activity who does not kill, does not intend that a death occur, and whose involvement in the crime did not cause the death.

   Answer (E) is incorrect because Answers (A), (B), and (C) are not valid crimes for the death penalty.

170. The Supreme Court allows the states great latitude in formulating aggravating and mitigating factors for the sentencer's consideration in capital cases, but there are limits. One such limit, premised on the Eighth Amendment's Cruel and Unusual Punishment Clause, is that the state must permit the sentencer to take an "individualized" approach that involves considering virtually anything relevant to mitigation. *Lockett v. Ohio*, 438 U.S. 586 (1978). This includes information about the defendant's background, character, and details about the crime that could convince the jury to impose a sentence other than death. *See e.g., Johnson v. Texas*, 509 U.S. 350 (1993) (jury must be permitted to consider youth of defendant as mitigating factor); *Penry v. Lynaugh*, 492 U.S. 302 (1989) (jury must be permitted to consider mitigating evidence about defendant's mental retardation and childhood abuse).

The instant defendant's childhood abuse by the priest would qualify as relevant to an individualized approach to mitigation and should be admitted.

171. **Answer (C) is correct.** A state may constitutionally allow a victim impact statement to be introduced as evidence in the sentencing phase of a capital case. *Payne v. Tennessee*, 501 U.S. 808 (1991). The Court condoned testimony providing the sentencer with a sense of the victim and the harm caused by the defendant, but prohibited testimony about the specific sentence that should be imposed.

Answer (A) is incorrect. In *Ring v. Arizona*, 536 U.S. 584 (2002) and *Hurst v. Florida*, 136 S. Ct. 616 (2016), the Supreme Court held that under the Sixth Amendment, a jury (unless waived) must decide any fact that increases the maximum punishment authorized by the jury verdict of guilt. In *Hurst*, the Court struck down a Florida law that required the judge to decide whether there were aggravating circumstances meriting the death penalty. The jury provided the trial judge with an advisory opinion. The Court held that Florida must give the jury (unless waived) the responsibility of deciding whether aggravating circumstances were present since the aggravating circumstances were deemed to be an "element" that exposed the defendant to greater punishment than permitted under the jury's guilty verdict alone.

Answer (B) is incorrect. The Supreme Court has invalidated state laws authorizing a mandatory death penalty. *E.g., Woodson v. North Carolina*, 428 U.S. 280 (1976). The determination to sentence a defendant to death must be based on the particular facts of the case and the defendant rather than on a flat rule mandating the penalty of death in certain types of cases.

Answer (D) is incorrect since all of the above are not true.

172. **Answer (A) is correct.** Retribution is not designed to prevent future conduct; its focus is on punishing someone because the person deserves to be punished for violating the criminal law.

Answer (B) is incorrect. Deterrence is designed to prevent (deter) future conduct by having the offender or people generally not commit crimes because of fear of punishment.

Answer (C) is incorrect. Rehabilitation attempts to change the offender's values/opportunities so he or she will not reoffend.

Answer (D) is incorrect. Incapacitation seeks to make it impossible for the offender to reoffend by removing the defendant from society (prison) or otherwise taking away the opportunity for continued criminal activity.

173. **Answer (C) is correct.** At allocution, the defendant may address the court concerning his or her views about the sentence. Rule 32(i)(4) of the Federal Rules of Criminal Procedure specifically gives the accused the right of allocation in a federal sentence proceeding.

Answer (A) is incorrect. Of course, defense counsel may address the issue of sentence, but this is not considered "allocution."

Answer (B) is incorrect. Allocution refers to a statement by the defendant, not by the jury.

Answer (D) is incorrect. The prosecutor may express sentiments about the appropriate sentence, but allocution refers to a statement by the defendant, not the prosecutor.

174. **Answer (A) is a correct statement** of the law. In *Apprendi v. New Jersey*, 530 U.S. 466 (2000), the Supreme Court held that "any fact that increases the penalty for a crime beyond the prescribed statutory maximum must be submitted to a jury." Later, in *Alleyne v. U.S.*, 133 S. Ct. 2151 (2013), the Court held that *Apprendi* also requires a jury decision on facts that raise the statutory minimum sentence.

Answers (B) and (C) are incorrect based on the case law just noted.

Answer (D) is incorrect. No case requires the jury to impose sentence in all cases where any statutory factor at all is used. Various factors, such as the facts of the crime itself, are routinely used in sentencing and do not need to be assessed by a jury; the judge alone may use these factors.

175. Rule 32 provides you with a means of protecting your sources for the presentence report. Under Rule 32(d)(3), your report "must exclude" "(B) any sources of information obtained upon a promise of confidentiality; and (C) any other information that, if disclosed, might result in physical or other harm to the defendant or others." This means that if you promise confidentiality for any of these sources, you do not have to disclose the source's identity. You may also delete any other information that might result in physical harm to your sources or

other people.

176.   **Answer (D) is correct** because interested members of the community are not entitled to speak at a federal sentencing hearing.

Answers (A), (B), and (C) are incorrect. Rule 32(i) specifically permits the defendant, defense counsel, and the victim to be heard before sentence is imposed.

177.   **Answer (D) is correct** because none of the above rules is followed in sentencing hearings.

Answer (A) is incorrect. The exclusionary rule barring evidence seized in violation of the Fourth Amendment does not apply at federal sentencing hearings.

Answer (B) is incorrect. Federal Rule of Evidence 1101(d) specifically provides that the evidence rules are inapplicable at sentencing.

Answer (C) is incorrect. The person being sentenced does not have the right to confront anyone providing adverse information.

178.   The primary argument is that the 25-year sentence is so excessive that it violates the proportionality standard in the Eighth Amendment. Though the United States Supreme Court has rendered a number of fractured decisions on the issue, the Court has made it clear that a sentence that is grossly disproportionate to the gravity of the crime and the culpability of the offender would violate the Eighth Amendment. *Graham v. Florida*, 560 U.S. 48 (2010); *Harmelin v. Michigan*, 501 U.S. 957 (1991).

According to *Graham v. Florida*, 560 U.S. 48 (2010), the general approach in assessing whether the sentence is grossly disproportionate is to first assess the gravity of the offense (here, very serious) and the severity of the sentence (here, also very serious). If this leads to an inference of "gross disproportionality," the court should compare the defendant's sentence with those received by other offenders in the same jurisdiction and with the sentences imposed for the same crime in other jurisdictions.

Defense counsel's argument that this particular sentence is grossly disproportionate will likely be rejected. The severity of the crime and the severity of the sanction are not so grossly disproportionate as to create the inference that would trigger further analysis. In addition, the Court has upheld even longer sentences for lesser crimes. Thus, in *Lockyer v. Andrade*, 538 U.S. 63 (2003), the Supreme Court upheld two consecutive sentences of 25 years to life for thefts of five videotapes worth $85 by a person with three prior felony convictions for violent felonies. The Court held the sentence was not grossly disproportionate so as to constitute cruel and unusual punishment. Similarly, in *Hutto v. Davis*, 454 U.S. 370 (1982), the court upheld a 40-year sentence for possession of marijuana with intent to distribute and distribution of marijuana. A 25-year sentence for possession of porn involving a very young child would not seem to be so grossly disproportionate as to violate the Eight Amendment.

179. **Answer (B) is correct.** A federal prisoner challenging a federal conviction by a collateral attack ordinarily would file a Motion to Vacate Sentence under 28 U.S.C. § 2255.

Answer (A) is incorrect because ordinarily federal habeas corpus is used by a state prisoner. Federal prisoners challenging federal convictions ordinarily use the Motion to Vacate Sentence, 28 U.S.C. § 2255. Although this remedy is often referred to as habeas corpus, this is incorrect terminology for federal prisoners' petitions for post-conviction relief.

Answers (C) and (D) are incorrect because state remedies are not used to argue that a federal constitutional right was violated in a federal criminal trial. The state courts would have no jurisdiction over Pit Bull's case.

180. **Answer (D) is correct.** A federal habeas corpus petition may be filed in the federal district where the petitioner is "in custody." If the state has more than one federal judicial district, the habeas corpus petition may also be filed in the federal district where the state trial occurred. 28 U.S.C. § 2241(d).

Answer (A) is incorrect because the initial federal habeas corpus petition is filed in the federal district court where the petitioner is in custody (or was tried); the matter would be filed later in Washington if the Supreme Court of the United States is ultimately asked to review the matter.

Answer (B) is incorrect because a federal habeas corpus petition is filed in federal, not state, court.

Answer (C) is incorrect because the location of the state supreme court is irrelevant in assessing where a federal habeas corpus petition is filed. The appropriate federal court is either the district court having jurisdiction over the location of the state prison or the federal court having jurisdiction over the location of the state court trial.

181. **Answer (A) is correct.** A second federal habeas corpus application is barred if the identical claim was presented in a prior application. 28 U.S.C. § 2244(b)(1).

Answer (B) is incorrect because completion of service of the conviction being challenged in the habeas corpus petition is not a prerequisite for the filing of a habeas corpus petition. The reason for filing the petition is to obtain release from that sentence.

Answer (C) is incorrect. The statute of limitations for federal habeas corpus for someone in state custody is one year, not six months, after the state judgment becomes final by the expiration of the time for seeking direct appellate review of that judgment. 28 U.S.C. § 2244(d)(1).

Answer (D) is incorrect because federal habeas corpus is specifically designed to permit an attack on a state conviction obtained in violation of the United States Constitution. 28 U.S.C. § 2254(a). It is not an appropriate remedy for violation of a state constitutional guarantee.

182.   **Answer (D) is correct.** None of the suggested items would be helpful. Federal law strongly encourages a petitioner to file only one petition that brings out all grounds for reversing a conviction. If, as in the instant case, the first motion to vacate did not mention a particular ground, 28 U.S.C. § 2255(h) establishes the general rule that the court should dismiss a second petition alleging the new ground. However, this provision also establishes exceptions where the second petition will not be dismissed but neither of those exceptions applies in this case.

   Answer (A) is incorrect. The fact that the issue was actually presented in the first petition effectively bars reconsideration in the second, absent several statutory exceptions not present in this case. 28 U.S.C. § 2255(h).

   Answer (B) is incorrect because a failure to present the issue in an earlier petition is specific grounds for a federal court to disallow it in a second petition unless the failure to raise the issue earlier is excused because the factual predicate for it could not have been discovered through due diligence and raises issues of actual innocence. 28 U.S.C. § 2255(h).

   Answer (C) is incorrect because the fact that the case law on point had been in existence over 20 years makes it hard to establish that the issue could not have been discovered by due diligence.

183.   **Answer (A) is the correct answer** (it is not an accurate statement of federal law). 28 U.S.C. § 2244(b)(2) specifically provides that a claim presented in a second or successor habeas petition that was not presented in a prior petition shall be dismissed unless the claim meets stringent exceptions to the rule. The general rule is that inmates can file one, and only one, habeas petition.

   Answer (B) is not the correct answer (it is an accurate statement of federal law). Any circuit justice or judge may issue a certificate of appealability authorizing an appeal of any issue. 28 U.S.C. § 2253(c)(1).

   Answer (C) is not the correct answer (it is an accurate statement of federal law). Ineffective assistance of state post-conviction counsel cannot be a grounds for granting the Writ, 28 U.S.C. § 2254(i), but the Supreme Court determined that in some instances, the failure of post-conviction counsel to effectively represent a person can serve as cause and prejudice to forgive any procedural default of a claim. *Martinez v. Ryan*, 132 S. Ct. 1309 (2012).

   Answer (D) is not the correct answer since Answer (A) is the correct answer.

184.   **Answer (A) is correct.** The statute of limitations is tolled while any "state post-conviction or other collateral review" is pending. 28 U.S.C. § 2244(d)(2). However, this time does not include a petition for writ of certiorari to the Supreme Court of the United States. *Lawrence v. Florida*, 549 U.S. 327 (2007). The statute of limitations would run one year from the date the state supreme court declined review and therefore the petition is untimely and must be dismissed.

   Answer (B) is incorrect. After *Lawrence*, the tolling in 2244(d)(2) applies only to state court litigation, not Supreme Court review of the state court litigation.

   Answer (C) is incorrect. Equitable tolling does not apply to a miscalculation of the statute of limitations or an uncertainty in the law. *Lawrence v. Florida.* Even if the error in calculation was predicated on the attorney's or inmate's belief about the statute of limitations calculation, this does not qualify for equitable tolling.

Answer (D) is incorrect. The statute of limitation in habeas is the same as the statute of limitations in any civil action. The statute of limitations operates to force plaintiffs to bring their legal claims to the courts in a timely fashion. A violation of the statute of limitations prohibits any review of the merits of the underlying litigation and even meritorious albeit late filings must be dismissed.

185.   Federal habeas corpus petitioners must satisfy the so-called "exhaustion of remedies" requirement in 28 U.S.C. § 2254(b)(1), which in general, means that the applicant must have pursued all available state remedies or have a satisfactory reason for not doing so. In reviewing the file, you must ascertain whether your client has "exhausted the remedies available in courts of the State." 28 U.S.C. § 2254(b)(1). In essence, this question is answered by ensuring that the petitioner presented the claims or issues to the state courts through all available state court processes including appellate procedures.

Federal habeas corpus law specifically provides: "[A]n applicant shall not be deemed to have exhausted the remedies available in the courts of the State, within the meaning of this section, if she has the right under the law of the State to raise, by any available procedure, the question presented." 28 U.S.C. § 2254(c). This provision will require you to determine what issues were appealed in state court and whether there are still any available state remedies to raise the issues you want to address in your habeas corpus petition.

Federal habeas corpus law also recognizes that the exhaustion rule need not be satisfied in two situations, both of which you may have to investigate if your review of the file and state law suggests the issue has not been "exhausted." First, no exhaustion is necessary if there is an "absence of available State corrective process." 28 U.S.C. § 2254(b)(1)(B)(i). You should explore what remedies are still available in state courts to raise the issues you want to pursue and then determine if those remedies are still available to Fuentes.

The second excuse for not exhausting state remedies is that "circumstances exist that render such [available state] processes ineffective to protect the rights of the applicant." 28 U.S.C. § 2254(b)(1)(B)(ii). This difficult standard requires you to determine whether the existing state procedures are somehow ineffective in protecting your client's federal constitutional rights. The results of this investigation will tell you which claims can be raised in a federal habeas petition and which claims must first be presented to the state courts before the claims can be reviewed in federal court.

186.   Federal habeas corpus law makes it difficult to obtain relief on an issue that was adjudicated on the merits in state court: "An application for a writ of habeas corpus on behalf of a person in custody pursuant to the judgment of a State court shall not be granted with respect to any claim that was adjudicated on the merits in State court proceedings unless. . . . " 28 U.S.C. § 2254(d). This statute creates a presumption that the state court judgment was correct and imposes the burden on the petitioner to show that the state court decision was not just wrong on the merits of the claim, but wrong either because the decision is "contrary to, or involved an unreasonable application of, clearly established Federal law as determined by the Supreme Court of the United States" or that the state court decision was predicated on an unreasonable determination of the facts. 28 U.S.C. § 2254(d).

The question under either "contrary to" or "unreasonable application" is not simply whether the state court got the answer wrong, but that the state court was unreasonably wrong in reaching its decision. This is a very demanding standard designed to give effect to the federalism and comity concerns implicated by federal court review of state court criminal judgments.

A challenge under the "unreasonable determination of the facts" is likewise very difficult. The petitioner is limited to the facts before the state courts and cannot add new facts to demonstrate that the factual resolutions by the state court were unreasonable. You will have to review the entire state court record, determine what factual conclusions you believe were incorrect, and then show, using the facts already in the record, how the state court's determination of fact were "unreasonable."

Because a *Miranda* issue involves both legal and factual components, it may be possible to challenge the state appellate court decision under all three issues in 2254(d).

187.   **Answer (B) is correct.** In *Anders v. California*, 386 U.S. 738 (1967), the Supreme Court held that counsel should not leave an indigent defendant unrepresented on appeal even when appellate counsel is convinced the appeal has no merit. The Court prescribed what is now called an *Anders* brief that requires appellate counsel to file a document briefly referring to anything in the record that might arguably support an appeal. Counsel may request to withdraw from the case after the brief is filed. The indigent client should be given a copy of the *Anders* brief, which the appellate court will consider in deciding whether to allow counsel to withdraw and to dismiss the appeal.

    Answer (A) is incorrect. Informing your client that you will file no documents may violate your indigent client's right to be represented by counsel. The better procedure is for counsel to file an *Anders* brief described above.

    Answer (C) is incorrect. A letter to the appellate court is inadequate to satisfy the indigent client's right to be represented by counsel. An *Anders* brief should be filed instead of a letter.

    Answer (D) is incorrect. Filing a brief arguing issues that you know are frivolous is not consistent with the requirements that counsel be both candid and not misleading. An *Anders* brief is the better choice.

PRACTICE FINAL EXAM: ANSWERS

MULTIPLE CHOICE

188. **Answer (C) is correct.** The Equal Protection Clause of the Fourteenth Amendment protects against discrimination based on ethnicity.

    Answer (A) is incorrect because entrapment would be close to impossible to prove since your client was actively selling marijuana when your client was approached by the officer, an act which shows a predisposition to commit the drug offense and would essentially preclude a successful entrapment defense.

    Answer (B) is incorrect. The First Amendment's guarantee of freedom of expression is not implicated by the illegal drug sale in the facts.

    Answer (D) is incorrect. Double jeopardy would not be a defense because the deportation is not considered punishment for the marijuana crime, so the accused would not be punished twice for the same offense.

189. **Answer (C) is correct.** The indictment, occurring after the complaint and preliminary hearing, would occur third.

    Answer (A), (B), and (D) are incorrect. The complaint occurs first, containing the formal charge. Fed. R. Crim. P. 3. The preliminary hearing occurs after the complaint. The indictment is third and the arraignment (plea to the indictment) is last.

190. **Answer (D) is correct.** In *Gerstein v. Pugh*, 420 U.S. 103 (1975), the United States Supreme Court held that a person arrested without a warrant must have a hearing before a judge to assess whether there is probable cause to hold the person in jail. Such a hearing ordinarily must occur within 48 hours of arrest. *County of Riverside v. McLaughlin*, 500 U.S. 44 (1991).

    Answers (A), (B), and (C) are incorrect since none is triggered by a warrantless arrest. An initial appearance (Answer (A)) is required after every arrest, with or without a warrant. Fed. R. Crim. P. 5. The grand jury (Answer (B)) and preliminary hearing (Answer (C)) have nothing to do with the status of the arrestee.

191. **Answer (A) is correct.** In *U.S. v. Salerno*, 481 U.S. 739 (1987), the United States Supreme Court upheld the federal Bail Reform Act's provisions permitting pretrial detention to protect the safety of a person. Neither the due process nor excessive bail provision was violated by the so-called "preventive detention" rule. State laws authorizing detention for similar grounds also do not violate the United States Constitution.

    Answer (B) is incorrect. *Salerno* held that preventive detention to protect the life of a potential government witness does not offend the Eighth Amendment.

    Answer (C) is incorrect. Due Process protection is not violated by a classification scheme permitting pretrial detention of persons who have threatened the lives of government witnesses.

Answer (D) is incorrect. The Bail Reform Act of 1984 regulates pretrial release of persons facing charges in federal court, not state court.

192. **Answer (A) is correct** (*i.e.*, it is not true). At a preliminary examination (or hearing) under the Federal Rules of Criminal Procedure and similar rules in many other jurisdictions, the standard is probable cause, not beyond a reasonable doubt. The judge decides whether there is probable cause to believe that a crime was committed and that the defendant committed it. Fed. R. Crim. P. 5.1(e).

      Answers (B), (C), and (D) are incorrect (*i.e.*, they are all true). The preliminary hearing is adversarial, the rules of evidence do not apply, and, of course, the defendant has the right to testify. The standard for a preliminary hearing is relatively low: probable cause. Fed. R. Crim. P. 5.1(e). It is not beyond a reasonable doubt (Answer (A), the standard for guilt or innocence); or clear and convincing evidence (Answer (B), a standard rarely used in criminal law, but is present under the Federal Bail Reform act for release pending appeal); or preponderance of the evidence (Answer (C), the standard used in civil cases and for criminal defenses in some locales).

193. **Answer (D) is correct.** Since **Answers (A), (B), and (C)** are all true, the best response is Answer (D), all of the above. Under the Federal Bail Reform Act, 18 U.S.C. § 3143(b), a defendant who seeks release pending appeal must establish by clear and convincing evidence that he or she is not likely to flee (Answer (A)) or pose a danger to the safety of the community (Answer (B)) and that the appeal raises a substantial question of law likely to result in reversal or a new trial (Answer (C)).

194. **Answer (B) is correct.** The United States Constitution does not mandate a grand jury and states are free to forego the procedure. *Hurtado v. California*, 110 U.S. 516 (1884).

      Answers (A), (C), and (D) are incorrect since under the United States Constitution states are free to adopt or reject in whole or part the use of grand juries. Some states have used this latitude and have eliminated the grand jury and substitute prosecution based on an information or complaint.

195. **Answer (B) is correct.** Even if the results of a lie detector were admissible at trial (which they are not in most jurisdictions), the prosecutor has no constitutional duty to share exculpatory evidence with a grand jury. *U.S. v. Williams*, 504 U.S. 36 (1992). Many commentators and a few jurisdictions disagree with this approach and argue that the prosecutor should provide known exculpatory information with the grand jury so the grand jurors have the data needed to perform their important screening function.

      Answer (A) is incorrect. Due process does not mandate that exculpatory evidence be given to the grand jury, even if that evidence would have convinced the grand jury to refuse an indictment. Due process is satisfied if the defense has a chance to provide this evidence to the petit jury at trial.

      Answer (C) is incorrect. The Fifth Amendment does not require the government to give the grand jury exculpatory information. Indeed, the grand jury itself is not even required in state criminal procedures.

      Answer (D) is incorrect. The defendant's right to present exculpatory evidence to a grand jury does not exist. It does not matter whether the exculpatory evidence was presented to the prosecutor or to the trial judge.

196. **Answer (C) is correct.** Rule 7(c) specifically provides that an indictment must contain the "essential facts constituting the offense charged."

Answer (A) is incorrect. An indictment is required for a felony unless the defendant waives indictment. If there is a waiver, the case may proceed by information. Rule 7(b).

Answer (B) is incorrect. Surplusage may be removed from an indictment only upon the defendant's motion, not by the prosecutor at any time. Rule 7(d).

Answer (D) is incorrect. The indictment may contain the defendant's legal name but this is not required for all crimes. If the defendant's name is unknown, the indictment may identify the defendant by the defendant's DNA profile. Rule 7(c).

197. **Answer (C) is correct.** Under Rules 8(ab) and 13, of the Federal Rules of Criminal Procedure, joinder of offenses is permissible if of the same or similar character, based on the same act or transaction, or connected with or constitute parts of a common scheme or plan. All three crimes seem a part of Robert's plan to sell cocaine and escape prosecution for it. The gun was available to carry out the threat to shoot the undercover agent if she testified against him.

Answer (A) is incorrect because the three crimes are quite different, not of the same or similar character.

Answer (B) is incorrect, though an argument can be made that the three are part of the same act of selling cocaine and avoiding apprehension.

Answer (D) is incorrect because under Rule 8(a), joinder here is permissible as part of a common scheme or plan.

198. **Answer (D) is correct.** Under *Brady v. Maryland*, 373 U.S. 83 (1963), the Due Process Clause of the Fifth and Fourteenth Amendment requires the prosecution to disclose to the defense "material" information that would be "favorable to the accused" on either guilt or sentence. This rule is based on the principle that a fair trial is more likely if such evidence is provided.

Answer (A) is incorrect. As noted above, *Brady v. Maryland* requires the government to provide the defense with certain helpful evidence. The defense need not reciprocate. Thus, the discovery rules are not identical for both sides and the Constitution does not require such parity.

Answer (B) is incorrect. This answer is similar to Answer (A) and is wrong for almost the same reason. *Brady* makes it clear that the legislature has some restrictions on limiting discovery in criminal cases. Due process, in general, does not mandate that the rules not be tilted against the defense, though at some point it may be that particularly one-sided procedures that considerably disadvantage the defense could violate due process. Some criminal procedure rules requiring the defense to provide pretrial notice to the prosecution of certain defenses, such as alibi and insanity, may be viewed as tilted against the defense but are nevertheless constitutional. But a rule that rejected all discovery would not be constitutional in light of *Brady v. Maryland.*

Answer (C) is incorrect. Due process does not mandate reciprocal discovery or being fair to both sides. It is a right of the accused, not the government. Its minimal requirements are that the prosecution provide the defense with *Brady* materials that are "material" and "favorable" on sentence or guilt.

199.   **Answer (D) is correct.** None of the theories in Answers (A)–(C) is likely to lead to a reversal of the conviction.

Answer (A) is incorrect because a one-year delay in itself would not support a due process violation absent more compelling information. The government has no duty to investigate a case and bring charges. *U.S. v. Lovasco*, 431 U.S. 783 (1977). Perhaps the due process argument would succeed if it could be shown that the defendant suffered actual prejudice from the delay and that the delay was caused by the government's desire to obtain a tactical advantage.

Answer (B) is incorrect. Though speedy trial protects against delays between the arrest or formal charges and trial, it does not reach the period between arrest and indictment. In addition, a six month delay is neither unusual nor a violation of due process absent far more compelling circumstances.

Answer (C) is incorrect. The statute of limitations regulates the period between the crime and formal charges, not the time between an indictment and trial. The latter is covered by speedy trial.

200.   **Answer (C) is correct.** The usual rule is that the venue for a crime is where the crime occurred. Here this would be Scott County.

Answer (A) is incorrect. Venue is not based on where the victim lives; it is based on the location of the crime.

Answer (B) is incorrect. Venue is not based on where the defendant lives, but rather on where the crime occurred.

Answer (D) is incorrect since Answers (A) and (B) are incorrect.

201.   **Answer (C) is correct.** According to *Richmond Newspapers, Inc. v. Virginia*, 448 U.S. 555 (1980), the First and Fourteenth Amendments give the press and the public a right to attend a criminal trial. This right is not absolute, however, and may be denied for important, specific reasons and only to the extent that is necessary to further the important interests mandating closure. In the exam question, no such reasons are given, no findings have been made, and no limited disclosure options have been explored.

Answer (A) is incorrect. Though the defendant does have a due process right to a fair trial, no case has been made that a fair trial is not possible without removing the press from the courtroom. Other options will assure a fair trial, such as sequestering the jury or limiting their access to the media.

Answer (B) is incorrect. Though the defendant may attempt to waive a public trial, both the public and the press also have a right to a public trial and the defendant's desire to waive that right is not dispositive and does not automatically override the interests of the public and the press.

Answer (D) is incorrect because the government does not have an absolute right to a public trial. For important, articulated reasons, a judge may totally or partially close a trial to the extent necessary to serve those interests.

202.   **Answer (B) is correct and therefore Answer (C) is incorrect.** The Sixth Amendment does not bar a jury of 10 in a state felony or misdemeanor case. *Williams v. Florida*, 399 U.S. 78 (1970). Therefore, the state's reduction in the number of jurors in a misdemeanor case does not offend the United States Constitution.

Answer (A) is incorrect. The United States Constitution's Sixth Amendment does not bar a jury of 10 in a state felony or misdemeanor case. *Williams v. Florida*, 399 U.S. 78 (1970). Therefore, the state's reduction in the number of jurors in misdemeanor cases does not offend the United States Constitution. The separation of powers doctrine is irrelevant because the three divisions articulated in the Constitution for the federal government are irrelevant for state government decisions. States are not free to set the number of jurors in all cases. A jury of less than six, for example, would violate the Sixth Amendment in the U.S. Constitution, even if it otherwise satisfied the state constitution.

Answer (D) is incorrect. The Due Process Clause of the U.S. Constitution is not offended by a jury of 10 people in a misdemeanor case. *See Williams v. Florida*, 399 U.S. 78 (1970).

203.   **Answer (A) is correct.** A judge in most locales may give a deadlocked jury an instruction called an *Allen* or dynamite charge, urging the jurors to continue deliberation but give weight to the views of other jurors. The charge is named after the federal case, *Allen v. U.S.*, 164 U.S. 492 (1896), which approved it.

Answer (B) is incorrect since the accused is entitled under state law to a unanimous verdict before a conviction is valid. Giving the decision to the side with an "overwhelming majority" would not satisfy the unanimity requirement.

Answer (C) is incorrect. Though the court has the discretion to declare a mistrial, this decision would not accomplish Judge Nobuku's goal of having the jury continue deliberations and possibly reach a verdict in the case.

Answer (D) is incorrect. The court may not replace sitting jurors with alternates simply because the sitting jurors could not reach agreement. The defendant has a right to have the case decided by the jury that was selected to hear it.

204.   **Answer (D) is correct.** In a jury trial, the Double Jeopardy Clause applies only after the jury is sworn. *Crist v. Bretz*, 437 U.S. 28 (1978). Here, the full jury has not even been selected much less sworn. Thus, the Double Jeopardy Clause does not bar the cancellation and rescheduling of the trial.

Answers (A), (B), and (C) are incorrect because, as noted above, the Double Jeopardy Clause does not apply until after the jury is sworn, which did not happen in this exam question.

205.   **Answer (A) is correct.** Even though a potential juror's exposure to pretrial publicity may merit further inquiry to ascertain whether the juror could be unbiased because of the information, that exposure by itself will not ordinarily result in the person being excluded for cause.

Answer (B) is incorrect. If a potential juror is being prosecuted for a criminal offense, that person will ordinarily be excused for cause. The potential juror's possible bias against the prosecution (anger at being prosecuted) or against the defendant (desiring to please the prosecution) is seen as so strong that the juror will be excused for cause.

Answer (C) is incorrect. A potential juror who is in a marriage-like relationship with the accused will be excluded for cause as unable to be unbiased in the case.

Answer (D) is incorrect. A potential juror who is close to the victim will be excused for cause as unable to be unbiased in the case. Here, the juror is the victim's Sunday school teacher, presenting a concern over bias.

206. **Answer (B) is correct.** Under Rule 15, Federal Rules of Criminal Procedure, depositions are limited to preserving evidence, and cannot serve simply as a basis for discovery.

Answer (A) is incorrect. Rule 15 does permit depositions in exceptional circumstances to preserve evidence; the rule is not a total ban on depositions.

Answers (C) and (D) are incorrect. Under Rule 15, depositions are severely limited and used only to preserve evidence. The fact that the witnesses may be important to the defense, alone, will not suffice. Similarly, the consent of the prosecution also will not satisfy Rule 15.

207. **Answer (D) is correct.** The defendant's presence or absence at the time the hearsay statement was made does not affect its admissibility under the Confrontation Clause.

Answers (A), (B), and (C) are incorrect because all are needed for the statement to be covered and admissible under the Confrontation Clause. Under *Crawford v. Washington*, 541 U.S. 36 (2004), a testimonial statement is admissible against an accused if the declarant is unavailable (Answer (A)), was subject to cross examination about the statement (Answer (B)), and the statement is hearsay (Answer (C)). Of course, if the statement is not hearsay, it also would not be barred by the Confrontation Clause, which reaches only statements that satisfy the test of hearsay.

208. **Answer (A) is correct.** There is no limit on the number of challenges for cause, which generally remove jurors who are unable to serve or appear incapable of being sufficiently disinterested.

Answer (B) is incorrect. Statutes or procedural rules routinely limit the number of peremptory challenges available to each side. For example, under federal law, each side in a capital case gets 20 peremptory challenges and in a felony case the government has six challenges while the defendants collectively have 10 challenges. Fed. R. Crim. P. 24(b).

Answers (C) and (D) are incorrect. Since answer (A) is correct and answer (B) is incorrect, both answers (C) and (D) are incorrect.

209. Under the Double Jeopardy Clause of the Fifth Amendment, "no person shall . . . be subject for the same offense to be twice put in jeopardy of life or limb." This means that if a person is convicted of a crime, he or she may not be convicted of the "same offense" in a subsequent prosecution by the same jurisdiction.

Whether two crimes are the "same offense" is determined by the *Blockburger* test, stemming from *Blockburger v. U.S.*, 284 U.S. 299 (1932). This test asks whether "each provision requires proof of a fact which the other does not." In the instant case, attempted murder and sending a destructive device are not the "same offense" since each crime contains elements not present in the other. For example, attempted murder requires an act designed to take human life, while sending a destructive device requires that the offender use the postal system to send a destructive device, whether or not the object is to take human life. Attempted murder may be accomplished without any involvement of the postal service, but section A-46 mandates the use of the mail but does not require the intent to kill.

The motion should be denied since the current prosecution does not offend the Double Jeopardy Clause.

210. A guilty plea involves the waiver of many constitutional rights. Accordingly, it must be handled in a way that documents that the plea and waiver were knowing, intelligent and voluntary. *Brady v. U.S.*, 397 U.S. 742 (1970). Compliance with Rule 11, Federal Rules of Criminal Procedure ordinarily satisfies this test.

In the exam problem, Rule 11 was virtually ignored and the plea should be overturned since there is no record that it was entered knowingly, intelligently, and voluntarily. There are many obvious problems under Rule 11. First, the court did not place the defendant under oath.

Second, the court did not personally advise the defendant of the many constitutional rights (such as the right to a trial, to confront adverse witnesses, and to have a jury trial) available and that would be waived if the defendant entered a guilty plea, and of such procedural requirements as the maximum and minimum possible sentence. Rule 11 specifically requires the court to apprise the accused of these matters.

Third, the court did not ensure the plea was voluntary.

Fourth, no factual basis was determined.

Fifth, if defense counsel did not discuss the plea and its ramifications with Williams, the Sixth Amendment right to counsel may have been violated. The issue would have to be further explored to assess exactly what counsel did because the transcript contains conflicting statements on the issue.

211. The court should reject the prosecution's *Batson* claim. *Batson v. Kentucky*, 476 U.S. 79

(1986), bars purposeful use of race-based peremptory challenges, which violate the Fourteenth Amendment's Equal Protection Clause. While subsequent decisions have extended the *Batson* rationale to intentional discrimination on the basis of gender and other identifiable or ethnic groups, none has extended it to bar the use of peremptory challenges to exclude better educated people or similar groups. If better educated people are entitled to any protection, it would be analyzed under the rational basis test. In *J.E.B. v. Alabama*, 511 U.S. 127 (1994), the Supreme Court applied *Batson* to gender-based peremptory challenges, but said the parties may still exercise peremptory challenges to remove members of a group subject to rational basis analysis. Here, the challenges are based on a history of involvement with moonshine, not on any racial or other suspect classification or even directly on affluence. The *Batson* challenge will fail. The defense has also offered a neutral explanation for its use of peremptory challenges. This, too, will cause a *Batson* challenge to be rejected.

212.   Your motion will likely fail. The Supreme Court has held that the government has no due process duty to preserve evidence, but cannot destroy or lose the evidence in bad faith. *Arizona v. Youngblood*, 488 U.S. 51 (1988). Here, if you could establish that the government lost the fingernail scrapings in bad faith, you could make a due process argument that the case should be dismissed.

Your effort will be hurt by the fact that the scrapings may have not had any "apparent" exculpatory value, as noted in a footnote in *Youngblood*. The government had the scrapings analyzed by a lab but nothing of value to either side was found.

You should try to find out how the scrapings were lost and whether there was ever any doubt by the police as to the accuracy of their own lab reports. While establishing bad faith is difficult, it is not impossible but more facts are needed than are presented in the exam question.

213.   This question raises two discovery issues. First, the defense is entitled to access government-generated forensic tests if they would be helpful to the defense on guilt or sentence. *Brady v. Maryland*, 373 U.S. 83 (1963). This means that if the government lab tests show that the bullet did not come from Davis' pistol, the government must give the defense the lab report. Your boss should make a specific request under *Brady* for any lab results.

The other issue is Rule 16, which creates a structure for reciprocal discovery of certain items. Rule 16 is triggered by a defense request. If the defense requests lab reports under Rule 16(A)(1)(F) and the government complies, the defense must then give the government copies of defense lab tests that the defense intends to introduce at trial. Since it is likely that the defense will want to introduce its favorable lab tests but does not want to disclose them to the prosecution before trial, the defense should consider not requesting lab reports from the government under Rule 16. Of course even if no such defense request is made, the defense is still entitled to helpful lab reports under *Brady*.

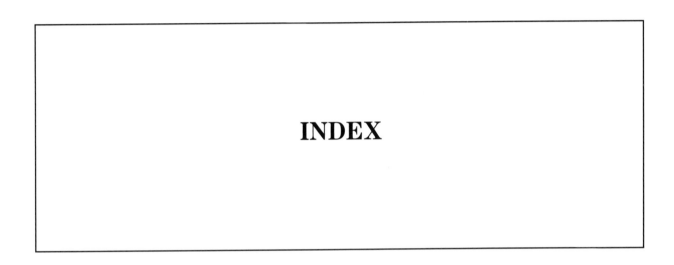

INDEX

INDEX